THE
DISAPPEARING
SPOON

THE DISAPPEARING SPOON

AND OTHER TRUE TALES OF RIVALRY, ADVENTURE, AND THE HISTORY OF THE WORLD FROM THE PERIODIC TABLE OF THE ELEMENTS

YOUNG READERS EDITION

SAM KEAN

Adapted for young readers by
Adrian Dingle and Kelsey Kennedy

LITTLE, BROWN AND COMPANY
NEW YORK BOSTON

The Disappearing Spoon: Young Readers edition was adapted for young readers by Adrian Dingle and Kelsey Kennedy. It is an abridgment of *The Disappearing Spoon* by Sam Kean, published by Little, Brown and Company.

Little, Brown and Company
Hachette Book Group
1290 Avenue of the Americas, New York, NY 10104
Visit us at LBYR.com

First Young Readers Edition: April 2018

Little, Brown and Company is a division of Hachette Book Group, Inc.
The Little, Brown name and logo are trademarks of Hachette Book Group, Inc.

The publisher is not responsible for websites (or their content) that are not owned by the publisher.

Library of Congress Cataloging-in-Publication Data
Names: Kean, Sam, author. | Dingle, Adrian, adapter. | Kennedy, Kelsey, adapter. | Young adult adaptation of: Kean, Sam. Disappearing spoon.
Title: The disappearing spoon: and other true tales of rivalry, adventure, and the history of the world from the periodic table of the elements / Sam Kean; adapted for young readers by Adrian Dingle and Kelsey Kennedy.
Description: First young readers edition. | New York, NY: Little, Brown and Company, 2018. | Audience: Ages 10+ | Includes bibliographical references and index.
Identifiers: LCCN 2017043585| ISBN 9780316388283 (hardcover) | ISBN 9780316388245 (library edition ebook) | ISBN 9780316388252 (ebook)
Subjects: LCSH: Chemical elements—Miscellanea—Juvenile literature. | Periodic table of the elements—Juvenile literature. | Science—Miscellanea—Juvenile literature.
Classification: LCC QD466 .K37 2018 | DDC 546—dc23
LC record available at https://lccn.loc.gov/2017043585

ISBNs: 978-0-316-38828-3 (hardcover), 978-0-316-38825-2 (ebook)

Printed in the United States of America

LSC-C

10 9 8 7 6 5 4 3 2 1

THE
DISAPPEARING
SPOON

CONTENTS

INTRODUCTION

AS A CHILD IN THE EARLY 1980S, I TENDED TO TALK WITH THINGS IN MY MOUTH— food, dentist's tubes, balloons that would fly away, whatever—and if no one else was around, I'd talk anyway. This habit led to my fascination with the periodic table the first time I was left alone with a thermometer under my tongue. I came down with strep throat something like a dozen times in the second and third grades, and for days on end it would hurt to swallow. I didn't mind staying home from school and medicating myself with vanilla ice cream and chocolate sauce. Being sick always gave me another chance to break an old-fashioned mercury thermometer, too.

Lying there with the glass stick under my tongue, I would answer an imagined question out loud, and the thermometer would slip from my mouth and shatter on the hardwood floor, the liquid mercury in the bulb scattering like ball bearings. A minute later, my mother would drop to the floor, despite her arthritic hip, and begin corralling the balls. Using a toothpick like a hockey stick, she'd brush the supple spheres toward one another until they almost touched. Suddenly, with a final nudge, one sphere would gulp the other. A single, seamless ball would be left quivering where there had been two. She'd repeat this magic trick over and over across the floor, one large ball swallowing the others until the entire silver lentil was reconstructed.

Once she'd gathered every bit of mercury, she'd take down the green-labeled plastic pill bottle that we kept on a knickknack shelf in the kitchen between a teddy bear with a fishing pole and a blue ceramic mug from a 1985 family reunion. After rolling the ball onto an envelope, she'd carefully pour the latest thermometer's worth of mercury onto the pecan-sized glob in the bottle. Sometimes, before hiding the bottle away, she'd pour the quicksilver into the lid and let my siblings and me watch the futuristic metal whisk around, always splitting and healing itself flawlessly.

Medieval alchemists, despite their lust for gold, considered mercury the most potent and poetic substance in the universe. As a child, I would have agreed with them. I would even have believed, as they did, that it housed otherworldly spirits.

Mercury acts this way, I later found out, because it is an element. Unlike water (H_2O), or carbon dioxide (CO_2), or almost anything else you encounter day to day, you cannot naturally separate mercury into smaller units. In fact, mercury is one of the more cultish elements: Its atoms want to keep company only with other mercury atoms, and they minimize contact with the outside world by crouching into a sphere. Most liquids I spilled as a child weren't like that. Water tumbled all over, as did oil, vinegar, and unset Jell-O. Mercury never left a speck. My parents always warned me to wear shoes whenever I dropped a thermometer, to prevent those invisible glass shards from getting into my feet. But I never recall warnings about stray mercury.

For a long time, I kept an eye out for element 80 at school and in books, as you might watch for a childhood friend's name in the newspaper. I'm from the Great Plains (South Dakota) and had learned in history class about the famous explorers Lewis and Clark and their trek through South Dakota and the rest of the Louisiana Territory. What I didn't know at first was that Lewis and Clark carried with them six hundred mercury laxatives, each four times the size of an aspirin. The laxatives were called Dr. Rush's Bilious Pills, after Benjamin Rush, a signer of the Declaration of Independence and a medical hero for bravely staying in Philadelphia during a yellow fever epidemic in 1793. His pet treatment, for any disease, was a mercury chloride sludge that he force-fed people, often until their teeth and hair fell out. (Be thankful that medicine is much better these days!) So how do we know that Lewis and Clark had them? With the weird food and questionable water they encountered in the wild, someone in their party was always queasy, and to this day, mercury deposits dot the soil in many places where the gang dug a latrine, perhaps after one of Dr. Rush's "Thunder-clappers" had worked a little too well.

Mercury eventually came up in science class. When first presented with the jumble of the periodic table, I scanned for mercury and couldn't find it. It is there—between gold, which is also dense and soft, and thallium, which is also poisonous. But the symbol for mercury, Hg, consists of two letters that don't even appear in its name. Unraveling that mystery—it's from *hydrargyrum*, Latin for "water silver"—helped me understand how heavily the periodic table was influenced by ancient languages and mythology, something you can still see in the Latin names that scientists use when they create new, superheavy elements for the bottom row.

I found mercury in literature class, too. Hat manufacturers once used a bright orange mercury wash to separate fur from pelts, and the common hatters who dredged around in the steamy vats, like the mad one in *Alice in Wonderland*, gradually lost their hair and wits. Eventually, I realized how poisonous mercury is. That explained why Dr. Rush's Bilious Pills purged the bowels so well: The body will rid itself of any poison, mercury included. And as toxic as swallowing mercury may be, its fumes are worse. They fray the "wires" in the central nervous system and burn holes in the brain, much as advanced Alzheimer's disease does.

But the more I learned about the dangers of mercury, the more—like William Blake's "Tyger Tyger, burning bright"—its destructive beauty attracted me. Over the years, my parents redecorated their kitchen and took down the shelf with the mug and teddy bear, but they kept the knickknacks together in a cardboard box. On a recent visit, I dug out the green-labeled bottle and opened it. Tilting it back and forth, I could feel the weight inside sliding in a circle. When I peeked over the rim, my eyes fixed on the tiny bits that had splashed to the sides of the main channel. They just sat there, glistening, like beads of water so perfect you'd encounter them only in fantasies. All throughout my childhood, I associated spilled mercury with a fever. This time, knowing the fearful symmetry of those little spheres, I felt a chill.

From that one element, I learned history, etymology, alchemy, mythology, literature, poison forensics, and psychology. And those weren't the only elemental stories I collected, especially after I immersed myself in scientific studies in college and found a few professors who gladly set aside their research for a little science chitchat.

As a physics major with hopes of escaping the lab to write, I felt miserable among the serious and gifted young scientists in my classes, who loved trial-and-error experiments in a way I never could. I stuck out five frigid years in Minnesota and ended up with an honors degree in physics, but despite having spent hundreds of hours in labs, memorizing thousands of equations, and drawing tens of thousands of diagrams with frictionless pulleys and ramps, my real education came from my professors' stories. Stories about Gandhi and Godzilla and scientists thinking they'd gone stark raving mad. About throwing blocks of explosive sodium into rivers and killing fish. About people suffocating, quite blissfully, on nitrogen gas in space shuttles. About a former professor on my campus who would experiment on the plutonium-powered pacemaker *inside his own chest*, speeding it up and slowing it down by standing next to and fiddling with giant magnetic coils.

I latched onto those tales, and recently, while reminiscing about mercury over breakfast, I realized that there's a funny, or odd, or chilling tale attached to every element on the periodic table. At the same time, the table is one of the great intellectual achievements of humankind. It's both a scientific accomplishment and a storybook, and I wrote this book to peel back all its layers one by one, like the transparencies in an anatomy textbook that tell the same story at different depths. At its simplest level, the periodic table catalogs all the different kinds of matter in our universe, the hundred-odd characters whose headstrong personalities give rise to everything we see and touch. The shape of the table also gives us scientific clues as to how those personalities mingle with one another in crowds. On a slightly more complicated level, the periodic table encodes all sorts of forensic information about where every kind of atom came from and which atoms can fragment or mutate into different atoms. These atoms also naturally combine into dynamic systems, such as living creatures, and the periodic table predicts how. It even predicts what corridors of nefarious elements can hobble or destroy living things.

The periodic table is, finally, an anthropological marvel, a human artifact that reflects all the wonderful and artful and ugly aspects of human beings and how we interact with the physical world—the history of our species written in a compact and elegant script. It deserves study on each of these levels, starting with the most elementary and moving gradually upward in complexity. And beyond just entertaining us, the tales of the periodic table provide a way of understanding it that never appears in textbooks or lab manuals. We eat and breathe the periodic table; people bet and lose huge sums on it; philosophers use it to probe the meaning of science; it poisons people; it spawns wars. Between hydrogen at the top left and the man-made impossibilities lurking along the bottom, you can find bubbles, bombs, toxins, money, alchemy, petty politics, history, crime, and love. Even some science.

PART I

MAKING THE TABLE:
COLUMN BY COLUMN,
ROW BY ROW

CHAPTER 1

GEOGRAPHY OF THE ELEMENTS

WHEN YOU THINK OF THE PERIODIC TABLE, YOU PROBABLY THINK OF THAT COLORFUL chart with many columns and rows hanging on the wall of your science classroom. You may have talked about it in class, and you may even have been able to use it during tests and exams. Unfortunately, even when you could use it, this gigantic cheat sheet may have seemed less than helpful! But the table and each box on it are full of secrets waiting to be decoded.

On the one hand, the periodic table seems beautifully organized, but on the other, it can sometimes look like a jumble of long numbers, abbreviations, and what appear to be computer error messages ($[Xe]6s^24f^15d^1$). So what does it look like with all the clutter removed? Sort of like a castle, with an uneven main wall and tall turrets on both ends. It has eighteen vertical columns and seven horizontal rows, with two extra rows below.

The castle is made of "bricks," but the bricks are not interchangeable. Each brick shows an *element,* or type of substance (as of now, it has 118 officially named elements, with a few more coming soon), and together they make up the table. If any of those bricks didn't sit exactly where it was supposed to, the entire castle would crumble. That's no exaggeration: If scientists determined that one element somehow fit into a different slot, or that two of the elements could be swapped, the entire "castle" would tumble down. They all fit together in a particular way.

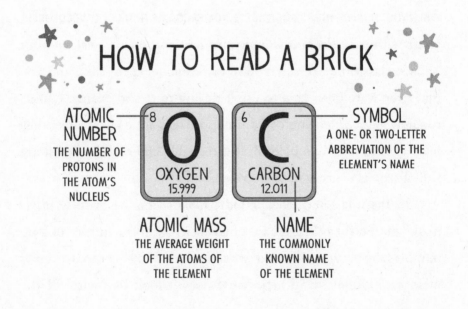

HOW TO READ A BRICK

ATOMIC NUMBER
THE NUMBER OF PROTONS IN THE ATOM'S NUCLEUS

8
O
OXYGEN
15.999

6
C
CARBON
12.011

SYMBOL
A ONE- OR TWO-LETTER ABBREVIATION OF THE ELEMENT'S NAME

ATOMIC MASS
THE AVERAGE WEIGHT OF THE ATOMS OF THE ELEMENT

NAME
THE COMMONLY KNOWN NAME OF THE ELEMENT

Seventy-five percent of the bricks are metals, which means most elements are cold gray solids, at room temperature. A few columns on the right contain gases. Only two elements, mercury (element 80) and bromine (element 35), are liquids at room temperature. In between the metals and gases, about where Kentucky sits on a map of the United States, lie some wacky elements that have crazy properties, such as the ability to make acids billions of times stronger than anything locked up in your school's chemical supply room.

What Exactly Is an Element?

The term "elements" goes back to ancient Greece. There, the philosopher Plato came up with the word (in Greek, *stoicheia*). Of course, Plato didn't know what an element really was in chemistry terms—he was using it to refer to air, water, earth, and fire.

Helium (element 2) is a good example of "element-ness"—a substance that cannot be broken down or altered by normal, chemical reactions. Today we say that carbon dioxide, for instance, isn't an element because one molecule of carbon dioxide divides into carbon (element 6) and oxygen (element 8). But carbon and oxygen *are* elements because you cannot divide them without destroying them.

It took scientists twenty-two hundred years to finally work out what elements actually are, simply because it was hard to see what made carbon *carbon* when it appeared in thousands of different compounds, all with different properties. It's kind of like the difference between chocolate ice cream and a chocolate chip cookie. They are both made with chocolate, but they are different in every other way (although they are both usually delicious). Nearly all elements form bonds with other elements to make compounds, and that makes it difficult to see what the pure elements themselves are really like. Scientists might have figured out what elements are much sooner had they known about helium, which exists only as a pure element and not in any compounds.

Helium acts this way for a reason. Each element is made up of a specific type of atom. All atoms contain negative particles called electrons, which live in different energy levels inside the atom. Each level needs a certain number of electrons to fill itself and become complete. In the innermost level, that number is two. Other numbers are required in other levels, but it's often eight. Elements have equal numbers of negative

IN 1911, A DUTCH-GERMAN scientist was cooling mercury with liquid helium when he discovered that below −452°F the system lost all electrical resistance and became an ideal conductor. This would be sort of like cooling an iPhone down to hundreds of degrees below zero and finding that the battery remained fully charged until infinity, as long as the helium kept it cold. A Russian-Canadian team pulled an even neater trick in 1937 with pure helium. When cooled down to −456°F, helium turned into a superfluid, with exactly zero resistance to flow. Superfluid helium defies gravity and flows uphill and over walls. Not even Plato would have predicted something so "cool" could actually happen in real life!

electrons and positive particles called protons, so they're electrically neutral because the positive and negative charges cancel out. Electrons, however, can be swapped between atoms, and when atoms lose or gain electrons, they form charged particles called ions.

Electrons are arguably the most important part of an atom. They take up virtually all of an atom's space, like clouds swirling around the nucleus, an atom's tiny core. If an atom were blown up to the size of a football stadium, the nucleus would be a tennis ball at the fifty-yard line.

What's important to know is that atoms fill their inner, lower-energy levels as full as possible with their own electrons, but when they undergo chemical reactions, they either lose, gain, or share electrons to secure the right number in the outermost level. Helium has exactly the number of electrons it needs to fill its only level, so

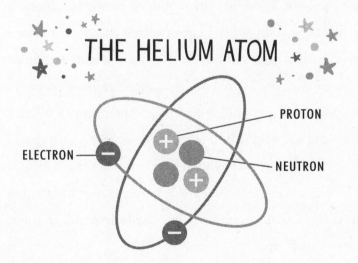

THE HELIUM ATOM

PROTON

ELECTRON

NEUTRON

there is no need for it to interact with other atoms or to lose, gain, or share electrons. This makes helium tremendously independent, possibly even "noble."

Electrons drive the periodic table, and no one did more to explain how electrons behave than American chemist Gilbert N. Lewis. Lewis spent his whole life working out how an atom's electrons work, especially in acids, and in their chemical opposites, bases. But one of the things he's best known for is that he was probably one of the greatest scientists never to win the Nobel Prize—and he was pretty bitter about it. Part of the reason he never won it is that he didn't discover anything that you could point to and say, "Wow! Look at that amazing thing!" Instead, he spent his life refining our understanding of how electrons work in many contexts, something that would help future scientists in a big way.

Before about 1890, scientists judged acids and bases by tasting or dunking their fingers into them—er...not a great idea or a very scientific one, either! Pretty soon, scientists realized that many acids contain hydrogen (element 1), the simplest element, which consists of just one electron and one proton. When an acid like hydrochloric acid (HCl) mixes with water, it splits into H^+ and Cl^- ions. Removing the negative electron from the hydrogen atom leaves just a bare proton, the H^+. Weak acids like vinegar pop a few H^+'s into the solution, while strong acids like sulfuric acid flood solutions with them.

Lewis decided this definition of an acid limited scientists too much, since some substances act like acids without relying on hydrogen. Instead of saying that H^+ splits off, he emphasized that Cl^- runs away with hydrogen's electron, like an electron thief. In contrast, bases (which, remember, are the chemical opposites of acids) may be called electron givers or donors. These so-called Lewis definitions of acids as electron pair acceptors and bases as electron pair donors emphasize the importance of electrons, and it fits better with the electron-dependent chemistry of the periodic table.

Although Lewis's acid theory is almost one hundred years old, scientists are still using his ideas to make stronger and stronger acids. You may know that acid strength is measured by the pH scale, with lower numbers on the scale like 1, 2, and 3 meaning stronger acids, and higher numbers like 12, 13, and 14 meaning stronger bases. In 2005, a chemist from New Zealand invented a boron (element 5)–based acid called a carborane, with a pH of –18 (yes, *negative eighteen*!). To put that in perspective, water has a pH of 7, and the concentrated HCl in our stomachs has a pH of 1. Because of the weird math of the pH scale, dropping one unit (e.g., from pH 4 to pH 3) boosts an acid's strength by ten times. So moving from stomach acid, at pH 1, to the boron-based acid, at pH –18, means that the boron-based acid is ten billion billion times stronger than HCl.

There are even stronger acids based on antimony (element 51), which has a colorful history. Nebuchadnezzar, a Babylonian king in the sixth century BC, unknowingly used a poisonous antimony-lead mix to paint his palace walls yellow. Perhaps not coincidentally, he soon went mad, sleeping outdoors in fields and eating grass like an ox. Later, around the nineteenth century, antimony pills were used as laxatives. Unlike modern pills, these hard pills didn't dissolve in the stomach, and they were considered so valuable that people rooted through poop to find and reuse them. Yuck. Some lucky families even passed (!) pills from father to son!

In fact, antimony was often used in medicine, since people didn't yet realize how toxic it was. Mozart probably died from taking too much of it to combat a severe fever.

We've come a long way in our understanding of acids and bases and how electron behavior drives the periodic table. But to really understand the elements, you can't ignore the part that makes up more than 99 percent of their mass—the nucleus. Whenever atoms react chemically, the nucleus remains unchanged, and only the electrons matter. Inside the nucleus, the number of positive protons—the atomic number, the whole number that's usually somewhere above the letters in each box in the periodic table—determines the atom's identity. In other words, an atom of one element cannot gain or lose protons without becoming an atom of an entirely different element.

And whereas electrons obey the laws of the greatest scientist never to win the Nobel Prize, the nucleus obeys the rules of probably the most unlikely Nobel laureate ever, Maria Goeppert-Mayer.

Maria Goeppert was born in Germany in 1906. Even though her father was a sixth-generation professor, Maria had trouble persuading a PhD program to admit a woman, so she bounced from school to school, taking lectures wherever she could. When she finally earned her doctorate, no university would hire her. She could enter science only through her husband, Joseph Mayer, an American chemistry professor visiting Germany. She returned to Baltimore with him in 1930, and the newly named Goeppert-Mayer began tagging along with Mayer to work and conferences. Unfortunately, Mayer lost his job several times during the Great Depression, and the family drifted to universities in New York and then Chicago.

Most schools tolerated Goeppert-Mayer hanging around to chat science. Some even condescended to give her work, though they refused to pay her, and the topics were stereotypically "feminine," such as figuring out what causes colors. After World War II, the University of Chicago finally took her seriously enough to make her a professor of physics. Although she got her own office, the department still didn't pay her.

Eventually she and her husband moved to a new university in San Diego that actually paid her a salary. By then she had discovered something called the nuclear shell model, which helped scientists understand the structure of the nucleus—but she still hadn't discovered a way to make everyone take her seriously as a scientist. When the Swedish Academy announced in 1963 that she had won her profession's highest honor, her local San Diego newspaper greeted her big day with the headline "S.D. Mother Wins Nobel Prize."

LOCATION, LOCATION, LOCATION

The position of each element on the table, which is determined by its atomic number (i.e., the number of protons), is crucial—its geography determines nearly everything scientifically interesting about it. So, in addition to visualizing it as a castle, you may think of the periodic table as a map.

First up, in column eighteen, at the far right-hand side, is a set of elements known as the noble gases. Many chemists find noble gases fascinating and, as with the idea of *elements*, we can trace this fascination with noble gases back to Plato. For someone who knew nothing about chemistry, he definitely had a big impact on it. If Plato had known what elements actually were, he might have selected the elements on the eastern edge of the table, especially helium, as his favorites.

Why? Well, in his writings, Plato said that unchanging things are more "noble" than things that interact with others. Helium and the rest of the noble gases tend not to react with other things, so Plato would probably have loved them.

Helium isn't the only element that has exactly the number of electrons it needs. The same idea extends down the entire eighteenth column beneath it—the gases neon (element 10), argon (element 18), krypton (element 36), xenon (element 54), and radon (element 86) all have the electrons that they need, so none of them reacts with anything under normal conditions.

The behavior of the noble gases is rare, however. One column to the west sits some of the most energetic and reactive elements on the periodic table, the halogens. Even more violent elements appear on the western edge, the alkali metals.

In addition to the reactive alkali metals on its west coast and halogens and noble gases up and down its east coast, the periodic table contains a "great plains" that stretches right across its middle—columns three through twelve, the transition metals.

As we move horizontally across the periodic table, each element has one more electron than its neighbor to the left. Sodium (element 11) normally has eleven electrons; magnesium (element 12) has twelve electrons; and so on. The addition of one electron to each transition metal would normally alter its behavior, as happens with elements in other parts of the table. But not those pesky transition metals. Chemically, many transition metals look and behave similarly. That's because, instead of exposing their outer electrons to the world (the way most elements do), transition metals often hide their outer electrons in a sort of secret compartment. As a result, transition metals tend to look the same to the outside world and behave the same way in chemical reactions.

Despite being normal metals in some ways, the alkali metals, instead of slowly rusting or corroding, can spontaneously combust in air or water. They also react easily with the halogens. The halogens have seven electrons in their outer layer, one short of the eight that they need, while the alkalis have one electron in their outer level and a full set in the level below. So it's natural for the group one metals to dump their extra electron on the group seventeen halogens and for the resulting positive and negative ions to form strong links. (When it comes to ions, opposites attract: Positive and negative ions are drawn to each other like magnets.)

This sort of linking—called ionic bonding—explains why combinations of halogens and alkali metals, such as sodium chloride (table salt, NaCl), are common. It's the easiest way for all atoms to get the electrons that they need. In a similar way, two ions of sodium (Na^+) take on one of oxygen (O^{2-}) to form sodium oxide (Na_2O). Overall, you can usually tell at a glance how elements will combine by noting their column numbers and figuring out their charges. Unfortunately, not all of the periodic table is so clean and neat. But the weird behavior of some elements actually makes them even more interesting.

CHAPTER 2

THE FATHERS OF THE PERIODIC TABLE

YOU MAY SAY THE HISTORY OF THE PERIODIC TABLE IS REALLY THE HISTORY OF THE many people who shaped it. Just as some of the elements of the periodic table are better known than others, many of the names of the scientists who discovered them and who arranged them into the first periodic tables are famous, while others have long since been forgotten.

BUNSEN, MENDELEEV, AND MEYER

One name from the periodic table's history that you may recognize is Robert Bunsen. This pioneer of the periodic table deserves special praise, since you've probably used a piece of school lab equipment named after him. Disappointingly, the German chemist didn't actually invent "his" Bunsen burner, but rather improved on the original design in the mid-1800s.

Bunsen's first love was arsenic, one of the most poisonous elements on the periodic table. Although element 33 has had quite a reputation since ancient times (Roman assassins used to smear it on figs and wait for their targets to eat), few law-abiding chemists knew much about arsenic before Bunsen started sloshing it around in test tubes. He worked mainly with arsenic-based cacodyls, chemicals whose name is based on the Greek word for "stinky." Cacodyls smelled so foul, Bunsen said, that they made him hallucinate. His tongue became "covered with a black coating." Perhaps from self-interest, he soon developed what is still the best antidote to arsenic poisoning, iron oxide hydrate, a chemical related to rust that clamps onto arsenic in the blood and drags it out. Still, he couldn't shield himself from every danger. The accidental explosion of a glass beaker of arsenic nearly blew out his right eye, leaving him half-blind for the last sixty years of his life.

Following the accident, Bunsen put arsenic aside and, after investigating geysers and volcanoes for a while, he settled back into chemistry at the University of Heidelberg in the 1850s. There, he invented the spectroscope, a piece of lab equipment that uses a prism and light to study elements. Each element on the periodic table produces sharp, narrow bands of colored light when heated. Hydrogen, for example, always emits one red, one yellowish-green, one baby-blue, and one indigo band. If you heat some mystery substance and it emits those specific lines, you can bet it contains hydrogen. This was a powerful breakthrough, as it was the first way to peer inside exotic compounds without boiling them down or disintegrating them with acid.

The only thing limiting spectroscopy at that point was getting flames hot enough to excite elements. So Bunsen created the device that made him a hero to everyone who ever melted a ruler or set a pencil on fire in a school chemistry lab!

Bunsen's work helped the periodic table develop rapidly for two reasons: First, the spectroscope allowed new elements to be identified. Second, and just as important, it helped sort through many claims for new elements by finding old elements in disguise in these unknown substances.

But beyond finding new elements, scientists needed to organize them into a family tree of some sort. And here we come to Bunsen's other great contribution to the table. At Heidelberg, he instructed a number of people responsible for early work in periodic law. This includes our second character, Dmitri Mendeleev, the man often referred to as the father of the periodic table. All the scientists working on early periodic tables recognized likenesses among certain elements. But some scientists were better than others at recognizing those similarities. Knowing how to recognize and predict such similarities soon enabled Mendeleev to create the first real periodic table.

Truth be told, like Bunsen and the burner, Mendeleev didn't conjure up the first periodic table on his own. At least six people invented it working independently, but Mendeleev became the most important character in the story of the periodic table. Born in Siberia, the youngest of fourteen children, Mendeleev lost his father in 1847, when he was thirteen. Boldly, his mother took over a local glass factory to support the family, but the factory soon burned down. Pinning her family's hopes on her smart young son, she bundled up Dmitri on horseback and rode twelve hundred miles across the mountains of Russia to an elite university in Moscow—which rejected Dmitri because he was born in a rural place. Undaunted,

Mama Mendeleev bundled him back up and rode four hundred miles farther, to his father's old college in Saint Petersburg. Just after seeing him enrolled, she died.

Luckily, Mendeleev proved to be a brilliant student. After graduation, he studied in Paris and Heidelberg, where Bunsen supervised him for a spell (the two clashed personally, partly because Mendeleev was moody and partly because of Bunsen's notoriously loud and foul-fumed lab). Mendeleev returned to Saint Petersburg as a professor in the 1860s and there began to think about the nature of elements, work that would culminate in his famous periodic table of 1869.

Many others were working on the problem of how to organize elements, and some even solved it. In England, a chemist named John Newlands presented his makeshift table to a chemistry society in 1865. At the time, no one knew about the noble gases (helium through radon), so the top rows of his periodic table contained only seven units. Newlands compared the seven columns to the do-re-mi-fa-sol-la-ti-do of the musical scale. Unfortunately, the Chemical Society of London thought this was a bit too childish, and Newlands was laughed at.

The more serious rival to Mendeleev was Julius Lothar Meyer, a German chemist with an unruly white beard and neatly oiled black hair. Meyer published his table at practically the same time as Mendeleev, and the two even split a prestigious pre–Nobel Prize called the Davy Medal in 1882 for codiscovering the "periodic law." While Meyer continued to do great work that added to his reputation, Mendeleev turned cranky and, incredibly, refused to believe in the reality of atoms and other things that he couldn't see, such as electrons and radioactivity. If you had sized up the two men around 1880 and judged who was the better chemist, you might have picked Meyer. So what separated Mendeleev from Meyer and the other chemists who published tables before them?

Unlike others who had tried arranging elements into columns and rows, Mendeleev had worked in chemistry labs his whole life and had a deep, deep knowledge of how elements felt and smelled and reacted, especially metals, the most difficult elements to place on the table. This allowed him to accurately place all sixty-two known elements into his columns and rows. Most important of all, while both Mendeleev and Meyer left gaps on their table where no known elements fit, Mendeleev, unlike Meyer, predicted that new elements would be dug up. Mendeleev even predicted the densities and atomic weights of hidden elements, and when some predictions proved correct, people were mesmerized. Furthermore, when scientists discovered noble gases in the 1890s, Mendeleev's table passed a crucial test, since it easily incorporated the gases by adding one new column.

Mendeleev threw together his first table to meet a textbook publisher's deadline. He'd already written volume one of the textbook but had covered only eight elements. That meant he had to fit the rest into volume two. After six weeks of procrastinating, he decided in one inspired moment that the most concise way to present the information would be to arrange them in a table. In it, Mendeleev not only predicted that new elements would fit into empty boxes beneath the likes of silicon (element 14) and boron but also provisionally named those elements. He used an exotic language to create those names, using *eka*, the Sanskrit word for "beyond." As a result, the "elements" eka-silicon, eka-boron, and so on were born.

THEORY VERSUS EXPERIMENT

Overall, Mendeleev's work in chemistry is comparable to that of Charles Darwin's in biology and Albert Einstein's in physics. None of those men did *all* the work, but they did the most work, and they provided more proof than others. They saw how far the consequences extended and backed up their findings with lots of evidence. And like Darwin, Mendeleev made lasting enemies because of his work. Naming elements he'd never seen was presumptuous, and doing so infuriated the man who discovered "eka-aluminium" and justifiably felt that he, not the Russian, deserved credit and naming rights.

Paul-Emile Lecoq de Boisbaudran was born into a winemaking family in the Cognac region of France in 1838. He moved to Paris as an adult, mastered Bunsen's spectroscope, and became the best spectroscopic scientist in the world.

In 1875, after spotting never-before-seen color bands in a mineral, Lecoq de Boisbaudran concluded, instantly and correctly, that he'd discovered a new element. He named it gallium (element 31), after Gallia, the Latin name for France. Some accused him of slyly naming the element after himself, since Lecoq, or "the rooster," is *gallus* in Latin. It took a few years, but by 1878 the Frenchman had produced a nice, pure hunk of gallium. Though solid at moderate room temperature, gallium melts at 84°F, meaning that if you hold it in the palm of your hand, it will melt (because body temperature is about 98°F). It's one of the few liquid metals you can touch without boiling your finger to the bone. As a result, gallium has been a staple of practical jokes. Since gallium molds easily and looks like aluminium, one popular trick is to fashion gallium spoons, serve them with tea, and watch people freak out when their spoon disappears into their drink.

Lecoq de Boisbaudran reported his discovery of gallium in scientific journals. It was the first new element discovered since Mendeleev's 1869 table, and when the Russian read about it, he tried to claim credit based on his prediction of eka-aluminium. The Frenchman and Russian began debating the matter in scientific journals, and before long, the discussion turned nasty.

Annoyed at Mendeleev's moaning, Lecoq de Boisbaudran claimed an obscure Frenchman had developed the periodic table before Mendeleev and that the Russian had stolen this man's ideas—a scientific sin.

For his part, Mendeleev claimed that Lecoq de Boisbaudran must have measured something wrong, because the density and weight of gallium differed from his own predictions. Lecoq de Boisbaudran soon retracted his data and published results that matched Mendeleev's predictions. According to science philosopher-historian Eric Scerri, "The scientific world was astounded to note that Mendeleev, the theorist, had seen the properties of a new element more clearly than the chemist who had discovered it."

The interesting debate here is theory versus experiment. Had theory tuned Lecoq de Boisbaudran's senses to help him see something new? Or had experiment provided the real evidence, and Mendeleev's theory just happened to fit? Although Lecoq de Boisbaudran denied he had ever seen Mendeleev's table, it's possible that he had heard of others or that the tables had gotten the scientific community talking and had indirectly alerted scientists to keep their eyes peeled for new elements. As no less a genius than Albert Einstein once said, "It is theory that decides what we can observe."

Of course, Mendeleev made many wrong predictions, too. He

was lucky, really, that a good scientist like Lecoq de Boisbaudran discovered eka-aluminium first. If someone had poked around for one of his mistakes—Mendeleev predicted there were many elements before hydrogen and swore the sun's halo contained a unique element called coronium—the Russian might have died in obscurity, but people tend to remember only Mendeleev's triumphs. Moreover, when simplifying history, it's tempting to give Mendeleev too much credit. He did a lot of the important work, but in 1869, only two-thirds of all elements had been discovered, and for years some sat in the wrong columns and rows on even the best tables.

YTTERBY, AN ELEMENT GOLD MINE

Loads of work separates a modern periodic table from Mendeleev's, especially one of the rows at the bottom of the table, the lanthanides. The lanthanides start with lanthanum (element 57), and their proper home on the table baffled chemists well into the twentieth century. Even Mendeleev, who wasn't shy about predictions, decided the lanthanides were too difficult to deal with. After cerium (element 58), he dotted his table with row after row of frustrating blanks. And later, while filling in new lanthanides after cerium, he often got their placement wrong, partly because many "new" elements turned out to be combinations of already known ones.

Mendeleev could have resolved all his frustrations had he traveled a few hundred miles west from Saint Petersburg. There, in Sweden, near where cerium was first discovered, he would have come across a nondescript mine in a coastal village with a funny name: Ytterby, pronounced "itt-er-bee," and meaning "outer village."

The Ytterby quarry supplied fine raw ore for porcelain and other purposes. More interestingly for scientists, its rocks also produced exotic pigments and colored glazes when processed. Nowadays, we know that bright colors are dead giveaways of lanthanides, and the mine in Ytterby was unusually rich in them for geological reasons. The Earth's elements were once mixed uniformly in the crust, as if someone had dumped a whole rack of spices into a bowl and stirred it. But metal atoms, especially lanthanides, tend to move in herds, and as the molten earth churned, they clumped together. Pockets of lanthanides happened to end up near—actually beneath—Sweden.

But while Ytterby had the proper geology to make it scientifically interesting, it still needed some great scientists to discover its treasures. The most important man in the discovery of the lanthanides was Johan Gadolin. Born in 1760, Gadolin was a chemist in a line of scientific-minded academics.

After extensive travel in Europe as a young man, Gadolin settled down in Turku, in what is now Finland, across the Baltic Sea from Stockholm. There he earned a reputation as a geochemist. Amateur geologists began shipping unusual rocks from Ytterby to him to get his opinion, and little by little, through Gadolin's publications, the scientific world began to hear about this remarkable little quarry.

Although he didn't have the chemical tools (or chemical theory) to tweeze out all fourteen lanthanides, Gadolin made significant progress in isolating clusters of them. He made element hunting a pastime, and when, in Mendeleev's old age, chemists with better tools revisited Gadolin's work on the Ytterby rocks, new elements started to fall out like loose change.

Gadolin had started a trend by naming one supposed element yttria, and in recognition of all the elements' common origin, chemists began to immortalize Ytterby on the periodic table. More elements' names (seven) trace their lineage back to Ytterby than to any other person, place, or thing. It was the inspiration for ytterbium (element 70), yttrium (element 39), terbium (element 65), and erbium (element 68). For the other three unnamed elements, before running out of letters ("rbium" doesn't quite look right), chemists adopted holmium (element 67), after the Latin name for the Swedish capital, Stockholm; thulium (element 69), after the mythic name for Scandinavia; and, at Lecoq de Boisbaudran's insistence, gadolinium (element 64), after Johan Gadolin.

Overall, of the seven elements discovered in Ytterby, six were missing lanthanides. History might have been very different—Mendeleev reworked his table constantly and might have filled in the entire row after cerium by himself—if only he'd made the trip west across the Gulf of Finland and the Baltic Sea.

CHAPTER 3

ALL IN THE FAMILY: THE GENEALOGY OF ELEMENTS

READING THE PERIODIC TABLE ACROSS EACH ROW REVEALS A LOT ABOUT THE elements, but that's only part of the story, and not even the best part. Elements in the same vertical column (called *groups*) are actually far more closely related to one another than elements in the same horizontal row (called *periods*). People are used to reading from left to right (or right to left) in virtually every human language, but reading the periodic table up and down, column by column, as in some forms of Japanese, is often more useful. You can discover some interesting relationships among elements, including some rivalries. The periodic table has its own grammar, and reading between its lines reveals whole new stories.

THE SAME BUT DIFFERENT

Elements in the same vertical column (group) are sometimes called a "family," since they are often very much alike. For example, both carbon and silicon have the same number of electrons missing from their outer level, which means they behave similarly in their interactions with other elements. Because carbon is the element most closely linked to forming life on Earth, silicon's ability to act like carbon has made it the dream of generations of science fiction fans interested in alternative—that is, alien—modes of life. At the same time, while carbon and silicon are indeed closely related, they are still distinct elements that form distinct compounds.

Directly underneath silicon on the periodic table, we find germanium (element 32). One element down from germanium, we unexpectedly find tin (element 50). One space below that is lead (element 82). Moving straight down the periodic table, then, we pass from the nonmetal carbon, the element responsible for life, to the metalloids silicon and germanium, elements responsible for modern electronics; to tin, a dull gray metal used to can corn; to poisonous lead, also a metal. Each step is small, but it's a good reminder that while an element may be similar to the one below it, many small changes add up to big differences.

One example of "the same but different" nature of Si and C is seen in their dioxides—compounds in which they combine with two oxygen atoms. Breathing in silicon dioxide, the major component of sand and glass, can cause pneumoconiosis—a nasty lung disease. Construction workers who sandblast all day and workers in insulation plants who inhale glass dust often come down with it. And because silicon dioxide (SiO_2) is the most common mineral in the Earth's crust, one other group is at risk: people who live in the vicinity of active volcanoes! (When volcanoes are the cause, this lung disease is sometimes referred to as pneumonoultramicroscopicsilicovolcanoconiosis, which is one of the longest words in the English language.) Our lungs regularly deal with carbon dioxide (CO_2), but absorbing its cousin, SiO_2, can be fatal. Many dinosaurs might have died this way: When a massive asteroid or comet struck the Earth sixty-five million years ago, it would have sent tons of poisonous SiO_2 into the air.

SMALL CHANGES BETWEEN ELEMENTS IN A FAMILY CREATE BIG DIFFERENCES IN HOW THEY FUNCTION

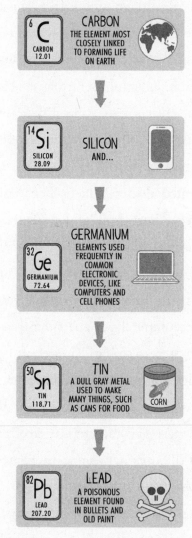

6 C CARBON 12.01

CARBON
THE ELEMENT MOST CLOSELY LINKED TO FORMING LIFE ON EARTH

14 Si SILICON 28.09

SILICON
AND...

32 Ge GERMANIUM 72.64

GERMANIUM
ELEMENTS USED FREQUENTLY IN COMMON ELECTRONIC DEVICES, LIKE COMPUTERS AND CELL PHONES

50 Sn TIN 118.71

TIN
A DULL GRAY METAL USED TO MAKE MANY THINGS, SUCH AS CANS FOR FOOD

CORN

82 Pb LEAD 207.20

LEAD
A POISONOUS ELEMENT FOUND IN BULLETS AND OLD PAINT

BLACK SHEEP

Every family has a black sheep, someone the other members of the family have more or less given up on. In group fourteen's case, it's germanium, a sorry, no-luck element found directly below silicon. We use silicon in computers, in microchips, in cars, and in calculators. Silicon semiconductors sent men to the moon and drive the Internet. But if things had gone differently sixty years ago, we might all be talking about Germanium (not Silicon) Valley in northern California today.

The modern semiconductor industry began in 1945 at Bell Labs in New Jersey, just miles from where American superinventor Thomas Alva Edison set up his factory seventy years before. William Shockley, an electrical engineer and physicist, was trying to build a small silicon amplifier to replace vacuum tubes in the massive mainframe computers of the time (these computers took up whole rooms, they were so big). Engineers hated vacuum tubes because the long, lightbulb-like glass shells were fragile and would overheat. Even though they despised them, they needed these tubes, because nothing else could amplify electronic signals (so that weak signals didn't die) *and* act as one-way gates for electricity, so that electrons couldn't flow backward in circuits. (You can imagine the potential problems if your sewer pipes flowed both ways.)

Shockley set out to do to vacuum tubes what Edison's lightbulbs had done to candles, and he knew that semiconducting elements were the answer: Only *they* could achieve the balance needed, by letting enough electrons through to run a circuit (the "conductor" part), but not so many that the electrons were impossible to control (the "semi" part). Shockley wasn't a very good engineer, though, and his silicon amplifier never amplified anything. Frustrated after two wasted years, he dumped the task onto two assistants, John Bardeen and Walter Brattain.

Bardeen and Brattain soon determined that silicon was too brittle and difficult to purify to work as an amplifier. Plus, they knew that germanium, whose outer electrons sit in a higher-energy level than silicon's and therefore are more loosely held, conducted electricity more smoothly. Using germanium, Bardeen and Brattain built the world's first solid-state (as opposed to vacuum) amplifier in December 1947. They called it the transistor.

This should have thrilled Shockley—except he was in Paris that Christmas, making it hard for him to claim he'd contributed to the invention (not to mention the fact that he had used the wrong element). So Shockley set out to steal credit for Bardeen and Brattain's work.

Hurrying back from Paris, Shockley wedged himself back into the transistor picture, often literally. In Bell Labs publicity photos showing the three men supposedly at work, he's always standing between Bardeen and Brattain, putting *his* hands on the equipment, forcing the other two to peer over his shoulders like mere assistants. Those images became the new reality, and the general scientific community gave credit to all three men. Shockley also banished Bardeen to another, unrelated lab so that he, Shockley, could develop a second and more commercially friendly generation of germanium transistors. Unsurprisingly, Bardeen soon quit Bell Labs. He was so disgusted, in fact, that he gave up semiconductor research.

Things turned sour for germanium, too. By 1954, the transistor industry was massive, but throughout the boom, engineers really wanted silicon and not germanium. Why? Well, in addition to conducting electricity so well, Ge generated unwanted heat, causing germanium transistors to break at high temperatures. More important, silicon was dirt cheap—in fact, as the main component of sand, it basically *was* dirt! Scientists were still faithful to germanium, but they were spending an awful lot of time thinking about silicon.

Luckily for Bardeen, his part of the story ended happily, if clumsily. His work with germanium semiconductors proved so important that he, Brattain, and, *sigh*, Shockley all won the Nobel Prize in Physics in 1956. Bardeen heard the news on his radio (by then probably silicon-run) while frying breakfast one morning. Flustered, he knocked the family's scrambled eggs onto the floor. It was not his last Nobel-related mishap. Days before the prize ceremony in Sweden, he washed his formal white bow tie and vest with some colored laundry and stained them green.

By 1958, the transistor industry faced another crisis. And with Bardeen out of the field, the door stood open for another hero.

Although he probably had to bend down (he stood six feet six), Jack Kilby soon walked through that door. Though trained in electrical engineering, Kilby was hired by Texas Instruments (TI) to solve a computer hardware problem known as the tyranny of numbers. Basically, though cheap silicon transistors worked okay, fancy computer circuits required lots of them. That meant companies like TI had to employ whole armies of low-paid, mostly female technicians who crouched over microscopes all day, swearing and sweating in hazmat suits, as they soldered silicon bits together. In addition to being expensive, this process was inefficient. In every circuit, one of those frail wires inevitably broke or came loose, and the whole circuit died. Yet engineers couldn't get around the need for so many transistors.

When Kilby arrived at TI, his bosses gave him free time to work on a new idea he called an integrated circuit. Silicon transistors weren't the only parts of a circuit that had to be hand-wired. Carbon resistors and porcelain capacitors also had to be joined together with copper wire. Kilby scrapped that separate-element setup and instead carved everything—all the resistors, transistors, and capacitors—from one firm block of semiconductor. It was a smashing idea—the difference between sculpting a statue from one block of marble and carving each limb separately, then trying to fit the statue together with wire. Not trusting the purity of silicon to make the resistors and capacitors, he turned to germanium for his prototype, which is now housed in the Smithsonian Institution.

Because the pieces were all made of the same block, no one had to solder them together. The integrated circuit allowed engineers to automate the carving process and make microscopic sets of transistors—the first real computer chips. Kilby never received full credit for his innovation, but computer geeks today still pay Kilby the ultimate engineering tribute. In an industry that measures product cycles in months, chips are still made fifty years later, using his basic design. And in 2000, he won a belated Nobel Prize for his integrated circuit.

Sadly, though, nothing could save germanium. Silicon was too cheap and too available, so it quickly replaced germanium. After germanium did all the work, silicon became the superstar, and germanium was largely forgotten.

PART II

MAKING ATOMS, BREAKING ATOMS

CHAPTER 4

WHERE ATOMS COME FROM: "WE ARE ALL STAR STUFF"

WE'VE LEARNED ABOUT HOW SOME OF THE ELEMENTS WERE DISCOVERED AND HOW they were organized, but where do elements come from? To answer that question, scientists had to figure out where *we* come from. The answers, of course, could be found in the periodic table.

THE BIG BANG AND OTHER THEORIES

The view that dominated science for centuries was that elements don't come from anywhere.

So, then, where did people think they came from?

Well, the thought was that the lifetime of every element was the same as the lifetime of the universe. They're neither created nor destroyed: Elements just are.

Later theories, such as the 1930s big bang theory, said that whatever existed back then, fourteen billion years ago, contained all the matter in the universe; everything around us must have started at that point. Not shaped like diamond tiaras and tin cans and aluminum foil yet, but of the same basic stuff. (One scientist calculated that it took the big bang ten minutes to create all known matter, and then joked, "The elements were cooked in less time than it takes to cook a dish of duck and roast potatoes.")

Over the next few decades, that theory began to be questioned. By 1939, German and American scientists had proved that the sun and other stars heated themselves by squashing two hydrogen atoms together to form helium, a process that releases a large amount of energy. Some scientists said, okay, the amount of hydrogen and helium may change (because of this reaction), but only slightly, and there was no evidence of the amounts of other elements changing at all. But as telescopes kept improving, data showed that most young stars contain *only* hydrogen and helium, while older stars contained dozens of elements. Plus, extremely unstable elements such as technetium (element 43), which doesn't exist on Earth, *does* exist in certain stars. The stars must therefore be making new elements every day.

In a mid-1950s scholarly paper, astronomers Geoffrey Burbidge, Margaret Burbidge, William Fowler, and Fred Hoyle explained a theory they called *stellar nucleosynthesis*. The paper, known simply as "B²FH"—which represents the last initial of each contributor—first suggests the universe was once a big mess of hydrogen, with a little helium and lithium (element 3). Eventually, hydrogen atoms clumped together into stars to produce helium. Only when the hydrogen burns up, B²FH suggests, do things start happening. It can be best described as evolution for elements—the paper explains how hydrogen, through various reactions, produces every element up to iron (element 26).

As a result of B²FH, once you've found iron in a star, you don't need to bother looking for anything smaller—once iron is spotted, it's safe to assume the rest of the periodic table up to that point is there, too.

You may think that iron atoms soon stick together in the biggest stars, and that the resulting atoms fuse together, forming every element on the rest of the periodic table.

Not so fast. When you do the math and examine how much energy is produced, you will find that fusing anything to iron's twenty-six protons *costs* energy. That means mashing iron atoms together does an energy-hungry star no good. Iron is the final element in a star's natural life.

So where do the heaviest elements—27 through 92, cobalt through uranium—come from? Ironically, says B²FH, they emerge ready-made from mini–big bangs, called supernovae. After burning through smaller elements, extremely massive stars (twelve times the size of the sun) burn down to just iron cores in about one Earth day. But before dying, these burned-out stars implode under their own immense gravity, collapsing thousands of miles in just seconds. In their cores, they even crush protons and electrons together into neutrons. Then, rebounding from this collapse, they explode outward, creating a supernova.

For one glorious month, a supernova stretches millions of miles and shines brighter than a billion stars. And during a supernova, so many gazillions of particles with so much momentum collide so many times per second that they high-jump over the normal energy barriers and fuse onto iron. Many iron atoms gain neutrons, some of which are converted into protons. Because the number of protons determines an atom's identity, new elements are created. Every natural combination of element spews forth from this particle blizzard.

One such supernova explosion created our solar system. About 4.6 billion years ago, a supernova sent a sonic boom through a flat cloud of space dust about fifteen billion miles wide, the remains of at least two previous stars. The dust particles mixed with the supernova and created a huge cloud. The dense center of the cloud boiled up into the sun, and planets were formed from the leftovers. But not only planets: the leftovers also include everything around you right now—books, walls, tables, food…everything. Even your own body was once part of a star. As the late astrophysicist Carl Sagan said, "We are all star stuff."

Two Types of Planets

The planets provided the names of many elements as well. Uranus was discovered in 1781, and despite the fact that it contains basically zero grams of the element, a scientist named uranium after it in 1789. Neptunium (element 93) and plutonium (element 94) followed from Neptune and Pluto. (Pluto used to be referred to as one of nine planets in our solar system, but as of 2006, it's no longer classified as a planet; it's now a dwarf planet.)

But of all the planets, Jupiter (a gas planet) has had the most spectacular run in recent decades. In 1994, Comet Shoemaker-Levy 9 collided with it, the first intergalactic collision humans ever witnessed. It didn't disappoint: twenty-one comet fragments struck the planet, and fireballs jumped two thousand miles high.

The history of our solar system's rocky planets (Mercury, Venus, Earth, and Mars) is different from that of the gas planets. When the solar system formed, the gas planets (like Jupiter) formed first, in as little as a million years. The heavy elements gathered nearby (well, relatively) and stayed quiet for millions of years more. When the Earth and its neighbors were finally spun into molten globes, those elements were blended more or less evenly inside them. In theory, you could have scooped up a handful of soil and held the whole universe, the whole periodic table, in your palm. But as the elements churned around, atoms began joining up with their twins and chemical cousins, until eventually large deposits of each element formed. Dense iron sank to the core inside each planet, where it rests today. When the Earth cooled and solidified, we were left with clusters of elements all over the planet.

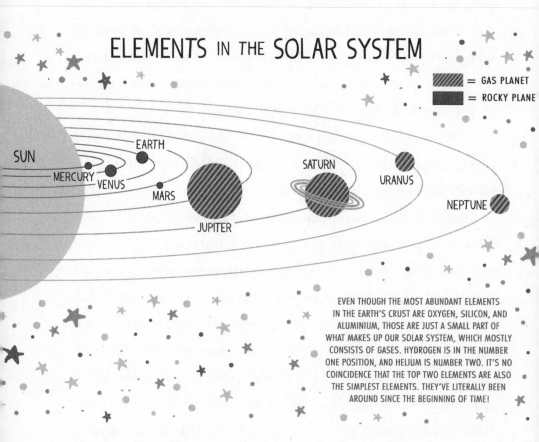

ELEMENTS IN THE SOLAR SYSTEM

▨ = GAS PLANET

█ = ROCKY PLANE

SUN

MERCURY
VENUS
EARTH
MARS
JUPITER
SATURN
URANUS
NEPTUNE

EVEN THOUGH THE MOST ABUNDANT ELEMENTS IN THE EARTH'S CRUST ARE OXYGEN, SILICON, AND ALUMINIUM, THOSE ARE JUST A SMALL PART OF WHAT MAKES UP OUR SOLAR SYSTEM, WHICH MOSTLY CONSISTS OF GASES. HYDROGEN IS IN THE NUMBER ONE POSITION, AND HELIUM IS NUMBER TWO. IT'S NO COINCIDENCE THAT THE TOP TWO ELEMENTS ARE ALSO THE SIMPLEST ELEMENTS. THEY'VE LITERALLY BEEN AROUND SINCE THE BEGINNING OF TIME!

ELEMENTS AND THE AGE OF EARTH

Given that our solar system's formation took place incomprehensibly long ago, reasonable people may ask how scientists have the foggiest idea of how the Earth was formed. Basically, scientists analyzed the amount and placement of common and rare elements in the Earth's crust and deduced how they could have gotten where they are. For instance, the common elements lead and uranium fixed the birth date of our planet through a series of insanely meticulous experiments done by a graduate student named Clair Patterson in Chicago in the 1950s.

Patterson used pieces of a meteor to figure it out, since meteors formed from the same dust the planets did, and have floated around in space unchanged since then. They are basically just hunks of the original Earth.

His findings? That our planet is roughly 4.55 billion years old. His experiments, which involved lead, also resulted in another important discovery: that lead levels in our atmosphere had been rising because of all the materials people were using it in (such as pipes, paint, gasoline)—and that this was bad for people and for our environment. Patterson became an important environmental campaigner, and he's the main reason future children will never eat lead paint chips and gas stations no longer bother to advertise "unleaded" on their pumps. Thanks to Patterson, it's common sense today that lead paint should be banned and cars shouldn't vaporize lead for us to breathe in. Trying to find out how old our planet is helped keep it (and us) healthy.

CHAPTER 5

ELEMENTS IN TIMES OF WAR

DESPITE SUPERNOVAE'S EXPLODING ELEMENTS IN ALL DIRECTIONS, AND DESPITE the best efforts of the churning, molten earth, some places ended up with higher concentrations of rare minerals than others. Sometimes, as in Ytterby, Sweden, this inspires scientific genius. Too often it inspires greed and destruction—especially when those rare elements find use in commerce, war, or, worst of all, both at once.

THE SCIENCE OF GOOD AND EVIL

Using chemicals as weapons started in ancient Greece, when the Spartans tried to gas Athenians into submission with the most advanced chemical technology they had at the time: smoke. It didn't work.

Chemical warfare progressed slowly for the next twenty-four hundred years, until World War I. By then, many countries recognized the threat of chemicals, and all the scientifically advanced nations in the world, except one, signed the Hague Convention of 1899 to ban chemical-based weapons in war. But the one holdout, the United States, had a point: banning gases that at the time were hardly more powerful than pepper spray seemed pointless if countries were still all too happy to mow down eighteen-year-olds with guns and sink warships with torpedoes and let sailors drown in the dark sea. Nevertheless, the other countries signed the Hague pact, and then promptly broke their word.

Early, secret work on chemical weapons centered on bromine. Bromine especially irritates the eyes and nose, and by 1910, military chemists had developed bromine-based chemicals so nasty that they could bring a grown man to his knees with hot, searing tears.

Since the Hague agreement concerned only warfare, in 1912, the French government decided to slow down a group of Parisian bank robbers with ethyl bromoacetate. Word of their capture quickly spread to France's neighbors, who were right to worry. When war broke out in August 1914, the French immediately lobbed bromine shells at advancing German troops. But they didn't have any more luck than the Spartans did. The shells landed on a windy plain, and the gas had little effect, blowing away before the Germans realized they'd been "attacked." However, it's more accurate to say the shells had little *immediate* effect, since hysterical rumors of the gas tore through newspapers on both sides of the conflict. The Germans used the rumors to their advantage, blaming one unlucky case of carbon monoxide poisoning in their barracks on the French, for instance. Their goal? To justify their own chemical-warfare program.

Thanks to one man, a bald, mustached chemist, the German gas-research units soon outpaced the rest of the world's. Fritz Haber had one of the greatest chemical minds in history, and he became one of the most famous scientists in the world around 1900, when he made a discovery that changed the world: He figured out how to convert the most common of chemicals—the nitrogen (element 7) in air—into an industrial product. When Haber invented a process to "capture" nitrogen, he was able to turn common air into ammonia, NH_3, the chemical used to make fertilizers. With cheap industrial fertilizers now available, farmers no longer were limited to compost piles or dung to nourish their soil. Even by the time World War I broke out, Haber had likely saved millions from starvation, and we can still thank him for feeding most of the world's 7.5 billion people today.

But Haber was interested in more than fertilizers. He actually wanted cheap ammonia to help Germany build nitrogen explosives. It's a sad truth that men like Haber pop up frequently throughout history—those who twist scientific innovations into efficient killing devices. Haber's story is darker because he was so skilled.

After World War I broke out, German military leaders recruited Haber for their gas-warfare division. Though set to make a fortune from government contracts based on ammonia, Haber couldn't throw away his other projects fast enough. The division was soon referred to as "the Haber office," and the military even promoted Haber, a forty-six-year-old Jewish man (who converted to Lutheranism to help his career) to captain.

Dozens of young chemists volunteered to work with Haber. Germany had fallen behind the French in chemical warfare, but by early 1915, the Germans had an answer to the French tear gas. The Germans tested their shells on the British army, not

DANGEROUS DISCOVERIES

Haber wasn't the first scientist whose discovery turned to destruction—and he wouldn't be the last. Here are a few others:

In the 200s BC, mathematician and inventor **Archimedes** supposedly used mirrors and the sun to send a "death ray" toward Roman ships, setting the attacking fleet on fire.

Swedish chemical engineer **Alfred Nobel** (yes, the prize is named after this guy) had been looking for a safe way to manufacture explosives. He succeeded in 1864 and called his invention dynamite, which was used to blast tunnels and create railways and roads all over the world. Of course, dynamite also went on to destroy as well as create.

Before **Werner von Braun** helped NASA launch its first satellite, named *Explorer 1*, in 1958, and develop the rockets that took the first people to the moon, he worked for the Nazis in his birth country, Germany. Pursuing his interest in space travel, he ended up helping to invent the V-1 and V-2 rockets, which the Nazis used as a weapon, killing thousands.

the French. Fortunately, as in the first French gas attack, the wind blew the gas away, and the British targets had no idea they'd been attacked.

The German military wasn't giving up and wanted to devote even more resources to chemical warfare. But there was a problem—that pesky Hague pact, which political leaders didn't want to break (again) publicly. The solution was to read the Hague pact in a bogus way. When they signed it, Germany had agreed to "abstain from the use of projectiles, the *sole* object of which is the diffusion of asphyxiating or deleterious gases." So to the cunning Germans, shells that delivered shrapnel *and* gas were okay. It took some engineering—the sloshing liquid bromine, which evaporated into gas on impact, was tricky to control—but Germany prevailed, and a fifteen-centimeter shell filled with a compound called xylyl bromide, another horrible tearjerker, was ready by early 1915. The Germans called it *weisskreuz*, or "white cross." Again leaving the French alone, Germany swung its mobile gas units east, to shell the Russian army with eighteen thousand *weisskreuze*. If anything, this attempt was more of a failure than the first. The temperature in Russia was so low, the xylyl bromide froze solid!

After two failures with bromine, Haber redirected his efforts to its chemical cousin, chlorine (element 17). Chlorine sits above bromine in group seventeen on the periodic table and is even nastier to breathe. Because chlorine is smaller—each atom weighs less than half of a bromine atom—chlorine can attack the body's cells much more easily. Chlorine turns victims' skin yellow, green, and black, and attacks their eyes. They actually die of drowning, from the fluid buildup in their lungs. If you thought bromine was unpleasant, then chlorine was a whole new level of nastiness. Enemy soldiers soon had to fear the chlorine-based *grunkreuz*, or "green cross"; the *blaukreuz*, or "blue cross"; and the nightmarish blister agent *gelb-kreuz*, or "yellow cross," otherwise known as mustard gas.

Not content with scientific contributions, in April 1915, Haber directed the first successful gas attack in history, which left five thousand bewildered Frenchmen burned and scarred in a muddy trench near Ypres. In his spare time, Haber also came up with a horrible biological law called Haber's rule to help calculate the relationship between gas concentration, exposure time, and death rate—which must have required a depressing amount of data to produce.

Despite having Haber, Germany ultimately lost World War I and was universally denounced as a scoundrel nation. The international reaction to Haber himself was more complicated. In 1919, before the dust (or gas) of World War I had settled, Haber won the 1918 Nobel Prize in Chemistry for his process to produce ammonia from nitrogen (the Nobels were suspended during the war). A year later, he was charged with being an international war criminal for his campaign of chemical warfare that had maimed hundreds of thousands of people and terrorized millions more—a contradictory, almost self-canceling legacy. He was never brought to trial.

Humiliated at the huge compensation that Germany had to pay to the Allies, Haber wasted six years trying to extract dissolved gold from the oceans, so that he could pay the bills himself. Other projects sputtered along just as uselessly, and the only thing Haber gained attention for during those years (besides trying to sell himself as a gas-warfare adviser to the Soviet Union) was an insecticide. Haber had invented Zyklon A before the war, and a German chemical company tinkered with his formula after the war to produce an efficient second generation of the gas.

Eventually, a new regime with a short memory took over Germany, and the Nazis soon exiled Haber for his Jewish roots. He died in 1934 while traveling to Palestine to seek refuge. Meanwhile, work on the insecticide continued. And within years the Nazis were killing millions of Jews, including relatives of Haber, with that second-generation gas—Zyklon B.

Modern Wars

While some elements such as bromine and chlorine have been used in war, other elements have caused (or at least assisted) wars—and not in the remote past, but very recently. Fittingly, two of these elements were named after Greek mythological characters known for great suffering. Niobe upset the gods by bragging about her seven lovely daughters and seven handsome sons—the easily offended Olympians then slaughtered the children. Tantalus, Niobe's father, killed his own son and served him at a royal banquet (reason: unclear). As punishment, Tantalus had to stand for all eternity up to his neck in a river, with a branch loaded with apples dangling above his nose. Whenever he tried to eat or drink, however, the fruit would be blown away beyond his grasp or the water would recede. Still, while elusiveness and loss tortured Tantalus and Niobe, it is actually a large excess of their namesake elements that has decimated central Africa.

There's a good chance you have tantalum (element 73) or niobium (element 41) in your pocket right now. Both are dense, heat-resistant, noncorrosive metals that hold a charge well—qualities that make them vital for cell phones. In the mid-1990s, cell phone designers started demanding both metals, especially tantalum, from the world's largest supplier, the Democratic Republic of Congo, then called Zaire. Congo sits next to Rwanda in central Africa, and you may have heard about Rwanda's terrible history of genocide in the mid-1990s, when hundreds of thousands of people were murdered. In 1996, the ousted Rwandan government spilled into Congo, seeking refuge. At the time, it seemed only to extend the Rwandan conflict a few miles west, but eventually,

HEAVY METALS

Three of every four elements are metals, but beyond iron, aluminium, and a few others, most did not do anything before World War II, except fill holes in the periodic table. But since about 1950, every metal has found a niche. Gadolinium is perfect for magnetic resonance imaging (MRI). Neodymium makes unprecedentedly powerful lasers. Scandium (element 21), now used as an additive in aluminium baseball bats and bike frames, helped the Soviet Union make lightweight helicopters in the 1980s and purportedly even topped Soviet ICBM missiles stored underground in the Arctic, to help the nukes punch through sheets of ice. Molybdenum and tungsten (element 74) are hard metals that can withstand high heat and when added to steel are made extrastrong. Even modest missiles tipped with tungsten were powerful enough to take down tanks.

nine countries and two hundred ethnic tribes were at war in the jungles.

Congo is a large country with dense forests, which make fighting a war difficult. Plus, poor villagers can't afford to go off and fight unless there's money at stake. Enter tantalum and niobium. Congo has 60 percent of the world's supply of the two metals. (In the ground they mix together to form a mineral called coltan; coltan is then processed to get pure tantalum and niobium.) Once cell phones caught on—sales rose from virtually zero units in 1991 to more than a billion by 2001—the West's hunger proved as strong as Tantalus's, and coltan's price grew tenfold. People purchasing coltan for cell phone makers didn't ask and didn't care where the coltan came from, and Congolese miners had no idea what the mineral was used for, knowing only that white people paid for it and that they could use the profits to support their favorite warring tribe.

Unfortunately, that wasn't even the worst of it. Unlike the days when crooked Belgians ran Congo's diamond and gold mines, nobody controlled coltan, and no fancy equipment was necessary to mine it. Anyone with a shovel could dig up whole pounds of the stuff in creek beds (like in the days of the gold rush). In just hours, a farmer could earn twenty times what his neighbor did all year, and as profits swelled, men abandoned their farms and growing food, and instead started looking for coltan. This upset Congo's already shaky food supply, and people began hunting gorillas for meat, making them virtually extinct.

But gorilla deaths were nothing compared with the human suffering. It can be dangerous when money pours into a country with no government. Without laws and clear rules for how that money could be used to help the Congolese population in general, a brutal form of capitalism took over in which all things, including lives, were for sale.

The worst times in Congo were between 1998 and 2001, at which point cell phone makers realized they were funding anarchy. To their credit, they began to buy tantalum and niobium from Australia, even though it cost more, and Congo cooled down a bit. Nevertheless, despite an official truce ending the war in 2003, things never really calmed down in the eastern half of the country, near Rwanda.

Overall, more than five million people have died in Congo since the mid-1990s, making it the biggest waste of life since World War II. The fighting there is proof that in addition to all the uplifting moments the periodic table has inspired, it has also been a source of some of the worst.

CHAPTER 6

COMPLETING THE TABLE... WITH A BANG

AS YOU LEARNED IN CHAPTER 4, A SUPERNOVA GAVE OUR SOLAR SYSTEM EVERY natural element, and the churning of young molten planets made sure those elements were well blended in the rocky soil. But that alone cannot tell us everything about the distribution of elements on Earth. Since the supernova, whole species of elements have gone extinct because their nuclei—their cores of protons and neutrons— were too fragile to survive in nature. This left holes in the periodic table—holes that, unlike in Mendeleev's time, scientists couldn't fill, no matter how hard they searched. They eventually did fill in the table, but only after developing whole new technologies that let them create elements on their own, and only after realizing that the fragility of some elements conceals a bright, shiny danger.

TIDYING UP THE TABLE

The roots of this story go back to the University of Manchester in England just before World War I. Manchester had assembled some brilliant scientists, including lab director Ernest Rutherford. Perhaps the most promising student was Henry Moseley.

Moseley grew enthusiastic about studying elements by blasting them with electron beams, although Rutherford objected to the work as a waste of time. In 1913, Moseley began to probe every discovered element up to gold (element 79). As we know today, when a beam of electrons strikes an atom, the beam knocks out the atom's own electrons, leaving a hole that other electrons rush to fill. All this crashing about causes the release of high-energy X-rays. Excitingly, Moseley found a mathematical relationship between the wavelength of the X-rays, the number of protons that an element has in its nucleus, and the element's atomic number (its spot on the periodic table).

Since Mendeleev had published his famous table in 1869, it had undergone a number of changes. Mendeleev had set his first table sideways, until someone showed him the sense in rotating it ninety degrees. Over the next forty years, chemists continued to mess with the table, adding columns and reshuffling elements, but some problems just wouldn't go away.

Most of the elements lined up on the table in a simple order of increasing weight. According to that method, nickel (element 28) should come before cobalt. But to make the elements fit properly— so that cobalt sat above cobalt-like elements and that nickel sat above nickel-like elements—chemists had to switch their spots. No one knew why this was necessary, and it was just one of several annoying cases. To get around this problem, scientists invented the atomic number as a placeholder, but no one really knew what the atomic number actually meant.

Moseley, just twenty-five years old, solved the riddle by translating the question from chemistry to physics. The crucial thing to realize is that very few scientists believed in the atomic nucleus at the time. Moseley linked an element's place on the table to a physical characteristic, saying that the positive nuclear charge was the same as the atomic number. This proved the ordering of elements was not random but arose from a proper understanding of atoms. Screwy cases such as cobalt and nickel suddenly made sense, since the lighter nickel had more protons and therefore a higher positive charge and therefore had to come after cobalt. After Moseley, there was no more need to fudge explanations.

Furthermore, like Bunsen's spectroscope, Moseley's electron gun helped tidy up the periodic table by sorting through a confusing list of radioactive isotopes (atoms of the same element with different numbers of neutrons and different weights) and disproving incorrect claims for new elements. Moseley also found four remaining holes in the table—elements 43, 61, 72, and 75. (The elements heavier than gold were too expensive to obtain proper samples to experiment on in 1913. Had Moseley been able to, he would have found gaps at 85, 87, and 91, too.)

ELEMENT HUNTERS

Tragically, Moseley was killed in World War I in 1915. (He had enlisted in the King's Army, against the army's advice.) The best tribute that scientists could pay to Moseley was to hunt down all the missing elements he'd pointed out. Indeed, Moseley so inspired element hunters, who suddenly had a clear idea of what to search for, that element safaris became almost too popular. Scuffles soon arose over who'd first discovered hafnium (element 72), protactinium (element 91), and technetium. Other research groups filled in the gaps at elements 85 and 87 in the late 1930s by creating elements in the lab. By 1940, only one natural element, one prize, remained undiscovered—element 61.

Oddly, though, only a few research teams around the world were bothering to look for it. One team, led by an Italian physicist named Emilio Segrè, tried to create an artificial sample and almost succeeded in 1942, but they gave up after a few attempts to isolate it. It wasn't until seven years later that three scientists from Oak Ridge National Laboratory in Tennessee announced that after sifting through some old uranium ore, they had discovered element 61. After a few hundred years of chemistry, the last hole in the periodic table had been filled.

Surprisingly, the announcement of the discovery of 61 didn't create much excitement, despite the name it received: promethium. A midrange element like promethium could no longer get people worked up like the heavy elements plutonium and uranium, not to mention their famous offspring, the atomic bomb.

To understand how subatomic particles behave, scientists had to devise a whole new mathematical tool called quantum mechanics, and it took years to figure out how to apply it to even the simplest hydrogen atoms.

Meanwhile, scientists were beginning to understand more about the related field of radioactivity, the study of how nuclei fall apart. Any old atom can lose or gain electrons, but great scientists, such as Marie Curie and Ernest Rutherford, realized that some rare elements could change their nuclei (their protons and neutrons), too. Rutherford helped classify these changes into just a few common types, which he named using the Greek alphabet, calling them alpha, beta, or gamma decay. Gamma decay is the simplest and deadliest—it occurs when the nucleus emits X-rays, and is today the stuff of nuclear nightmares. In beta decays, atoms released electrons, while in alpha decay, they released chunks of the nucleus. Beta and alpha radioactivity also involved the conversion of one element to another, a tantalizing process in the 1920s. But each element goes radioactive in a characteristic way, so scientists were confused and increasingly frustrated about the nature of isotopes as well.

The giant collective forehead slap—the "Of course!" moment—took place in 1932, when James Chadwick, yet another of Rutherford's students, discovered the neutral neutron, which adds weight to the nucleus without adding charge. Coupled with Moseley's explanation of atomic number, atoms suddenly made more sense. The neutron meant that you could have different forms of an element: They would have different atomic weights but would still have the same positive nuclear charge and sit in the same box on the periodic table. The nature of radioactivity suddenly made sense, too. Beta decay was understood as the conversion of neutrons to protons—and it's because the proton number changes that beta decay converts an atom into a different element. Alpha decay also converts elements and is the most dramatic change on a nuclear level—two neutrons and two protons are taken away.

Neutrons also helped scientists understand a new type of reaction. Elements, especially lighter elements, try to maintain a rough one-to-one ratio of neutrons to protons. If an atom has too many neutrons, it splits itself, releasing energy and excess neutrons in the process. Nearby atoms can then absorb those neutrons, at which point they become unstable and split. This split releases more energy and more neutrons, which makes even more atoms unstable, so that they split and release still more energy. If you release enough energy, this process—called a chain reaction—will result in a nuclear explosion.

Just as the basic understanding of electrons, protons, and neutrons fell into place, the old-world political order was disintegrating and World War II was about to begin.

With their new model of atoms, scientists began to see that the few undiscovered elements on the periodic table were undiscovered because they were unstable—they decayed away. Even if they had existed in abundance on the early Earth, they had long since disintegrated. This conveniently explained the holes in the periodic table. Probing unstable elements soon led scientists to stumble onto nuclear fission and neutron chain reactions. And as soon as they understood that atoms could be split (fission), simply collecting new elements for display seemed like an amateur's hobby. Which is why, with a world war and the possibility of atomic bombs staring at them in 1939, no scientists bothered tracking promethium down until a decade later.

THE MONTE CARLO METHOD

No matter how excited scientists got about the possibility of fission bombs, however, a lot of work still separated the theory from the reality. It's hard to remember today, but nuclear bombs were considered a long shot at best, especially by military experts. Figuring out how to divide atoms in a controlled manner proved so difficult, and so far beyond the science of the day, that the US government research into nuclear weapons (the Manhattan Project) had to adopt a whole new strategy to succeed—the Monte Carlo method. This method involved running simulations on paper instead of actually doing experiments, and it eventually changed what "doing science" meant.

As noted, quantum mechanics worked fine for very simple atoms, and by 1940, scientists knew that absorbing a neutron made an atom explode and possibly release more neutrons. Following the path of one given neutron was easy, no harder than following a soccer ball on a field. But imagine trying to follow a hundred or even a thousand soccer balls bouncing around all at once—it's much harder! Following chain reactions were even worse, because that required following billions of billions of neutrons, all of them traveling at different speeds in every direction. At the same time, uranium and plutonium were expensive and dangerous, so detailed experimental work was out of the question.

Manhattan Project scientists had orders to figure out exactly how much plutonium and uranium were needed to create a bomb: Too little and the bomb would fizzle out. Too much and the bomb would blow up just fine, but at the cost of prolonging the war by months, since both elements were monstrously complicated to purify (or, in plutonium's case: make, then purify). So, just to get by, some scientists decided to forget the usual approaches of theory or experiment, and find a new, third scientific method.

Basically, scientists used millions of pencil-and-paper calculations to collect only virtual data (not data from real experiments) for the plutonium and uranium bombs.

Of course, such calculations were only as good as scientists' equations, but here they got lucky. The sheer number of calculations scientists pushed through during the Manhattan Project gave them great confidence—confidence that was proved justified after the first successful nuclear bomb test in New Mexico in mid-1945. Then, the swift and flawless detonation of a uranium bomb over Hiroshima and a plutonium bomb over Nagasaki a few days later also testified to the accuracy of this unconventional, calculation-based approach to science.

After the Manhattan Project ended, scientists scattered back to their homes to reflect on what they'd done (some proudly, some not). Many gladly forgot about their time in the project. Some, though, were excited by what they'd learned, including one Stanislaw Ulam. Ulam, a Polish refugee who'd passed hours in New Mexico playing card games, was playing solitaire one day in 1946 when he began wondering about the odds of winning any randomly dealt hand. Ulam recognized that he was using the same basic approach as scientists had used in the bomb-building "experiments" in Los Alamos. Discussions soon followed with his calculation-loving friend

John von Neumann, another European refugee and Manhattan Project scientist. Ulam and von Neumann realized just how powerful the method might be if they could apply it to other situations. Unlike with an experiment, the results were not certain. But with enough calculations, they could be pretty sure of the probabilities.

So-called Monte Carlo science (since it was based on the probability used in the famous casinos) caught on quickly. It cut down on expensive experiments, and the need for high-quality Monte Carlo simulators (which ran equations instead of experiments) drove the early development of computers, pushing them to become faster and more efficient.

TYPES OF NUCLEAR BOMBS

In those early days, Ulam's Monte Carlo method mostly pushed through the next generation of nuclear weapons. Von Neumann and Ulam would show up at the gymnasium-sized rooms where computers were set up and mysteriously ask if they could run a few programs, starting at midnight and running until morning. The weapons they developed during those dead hours were the "supers," multistage nuclear bombs a thousand times more powerful than standard A-bombs.

After a great struggle to find the proper design for a super, scientists finally found one in 1952. The Eniwetok Atoll (a small group of islands in the Pacific Ocean) was wiped out during a test of a super, showing once again the ruthless brilliance of the Monte Carlo method. Nevertheless, bomb scientists already had something even worse than even the supers in the pipeline.

Atomic bombs can get you two ways. A madman who just wants lots of people dead and lots of buildings flattened can stick with a conventional bomb. It's easier to build, and the big flash-bang and aftereffects, such as spontaneous tornadoes and the silhouettes of victims seared onto brick walls, will do the job. But if the madman has patience and wants to do something much more terrifying, then he'll detonate a cobalt-60 dirty bomb.

Conventional nuclear bombs kill with heat, but dirty bombs kill with gamma radiation—dangerous X-rays. As well as burning people frightfully, gamma rays dig down into bone marrow and scramble the chromosomes in white blood cells. The cells either die outright, grow cancerous, or grow uncontrollably and end up deformed and unable to fight infections. All nuclear bombs release some radiation, but with dirty bombs, the terrifying radiation is the whole point.

Another European refugee who worked on the Manhattan Project, Leo Szilard, calculated in 1950 that sprinkling a tenth of an ounce of cobalt-60 on every square mile of Earth would pollute it with enough gamma rays to wipe out the human race. His bomb consisted of a multistage warhead surrounded by a jacket of cobalt-59. In the bomb, cobalt atoms would collect neutrons from the fission and fusion, a step called "salting." The salting would convert stable cobalt-59 into unsteady cobalt-60, which would then float down like ash.

Lots of other elements emit gamma rays, but there's something special about cobalt. Regular A-bombs can be waited out in underground shelters, since most of the radioactive atoms they release end up decaying quickly. Hiroshima and Nagasaki were more or less safe within days of the 1945 explosions. Other elements absorb extra neutrons and also turn radioactive, but because they decay so slowly after the initial blast, radiation levels never climb too high.

Cobalt bombs fall between those extremes. Cobalt-60 atoms would settle into the ground like tiny land mines. Enough would go off right away to make it necessary to flee, but after five years, half of the cobalt would still be waiting to release deadly radiation. The steady pulse of gamma rays would mean that cobalt bombs could be neither waited out nor endured. It would take a whole human lifetime for the land to recover. This actually makes cobalt bombs useless weapons for war, because the conquering army couldn't occupy the land that they had devastated since it would be too dangerous. But a madman, intent only on wiping out the human race, wouldn't care about that.

Szilard hoped his cobalt bomb—the first "doomsday device"— would never be built, and no country (as far as the public knows) has ever tried. In fact, Szilard came up with the idea to show the insanity of nuclear war. Before Szilard, nuclear weapons were horrifying but not necessarily so frightening that they could result in the end of the world. After showing the world the cobalt-60 bomb, Szilard hoped that people would know better and give up nukes.

Hardly.

Not long after the haunting name "promethium" became official, the Soviet Union acquired the bomb, too. The US and Soviet governments soon accepted the less-than-reassuring but aptly named idea of MAD, or *mutual assured destruction*—the idea that, whatever happened during a nuclear war, both sides would lose because of the devastation left behind. However crazy MAD seemed, it did stop people from using nukes as tactical weapons. Instead, international tensions gave birth to the Cold War between the United States and the Soviet Union—a struggle that so affected all of our society that not even the beautiful periodic table could escape.

CHAPTER 7

COMPETITIVE ELEMENTS: EXTENDING THE TABLE, EXPANDING THE COLD WAR

In 1950, an odd notice appeared in the magazine the *New Yorker*;

> New atoms are turning up with spectacular, if not down-right alarming frequency nowadays, and the University of California at Berkeley, whose scientists have discovered elements 97 and 98, has christened them berkelium and californium respectively.... These names strike us as indicating a surprising lack of public-relations foresight.... California's busy scientists will undoubtedly come up with another atom or two one

of these days, and the university…has lost forever the chance of immortalizing itself in the atomic tables with some such sequence as universitium (97), ofium (98), californium (99), berkelium (100).

Not to be outwitted by magazine writers, scientists at Berkeley, led by Glenn Seaborg and Albert Ghiorso, replied that their chosen names were designed to avoid "the appalling possibility that after naming 97 and 98 'universitium' and 'ofium,' some New Yorker might follow with the discovery of 99 and 100 and apply the names 'newium' and 'yorkium.'"

The *New Yorker* staff answered, "We are already at work in our office laboratories on 'newium' and 'yorkium.' So far we just have the names."

This was a fun time to be a Berkeley scientist. They were creating the first new elements in our solar system since the supernova kicked everything off billions of years before. No one could foresee how bitter the creation (and even the naming) of these elements would soon become—a new twist in the Cold War between the Soviets and the Americans.

MADE IN AMERICA

In 1940, Seaborg's colleague and friend Edwin McMillan captured a long-standing prize by creating the first element heavier than uranium, which he named neptunium, after the planet beyond Uranus, for which uranium had been named. Hungry to do more, McMillan realized that element 93 was pretty wobbly and might decay into element 94 by converting a neutron to a proton. He searched for evidence of the next element and kept young Seaborg in the loop.

But more was happening in 1940 than just the discovery of new elements. Once the US government decided to join in World War II, it began taking its scientific stars, including McMillan, and putting them to work on military projects, such as radar. Not yet famous enough to be selected for that work, Seaborg found himself alone in Berkeley with McMillan's equipment and full knowledge of how McMillan had planned to proceed.

Hurriedly, fearing it might be their one shot at fame, Seaborg and a colleague obtained a microscopic sample of element 93. After letting the neptunium decay, they sifted through the radioactive sample by dissolving away the excess neptunium until only a small bit of chemical remained. They proved that the remaining atoms had to be element 94 by ripping electron after electron off with a powerful chemical until the atoms held a higher electric charge (+7) than any ion ever known. From its very first moments, element 94 seemed special. Continuing the march to the edge of the solar system, the scientists named it plutonium after Pluto, the next planet in the solar system at the time.

Suddenly a star himself, Seaborg was summoned to Chicago in 1942 to work for a branch of the Manhattan Project. He brought students with him, plus a technician named Albert Ghiorso. When the pair returned to Berkeley after the war, they began to produce heavy elements, as the *New Yorker* said, "with spectacular, if not downright alarming frequency." Ghiorso and Seaborg discovered more elements than anyone in history and extended the periodic table by almost one-sixth.

The collaboration started in 1946, when the Seaborg-Ghiorso team messed around with plutonium and ended up making elements 95 and 96, which earned them the right to name their discoveries. They selected americium (pronounced "am-er-EE-see-um"), after America, and curium, after Marie Curie. Seaborg announced the elements not in a scientific journal but on a children's radio show, *Quiz Kids*. One kid asked Mr. Seaborg if (ha, ha) he'd discovered any new elements lately. Seaborg answered that he had, actually, and encouraged kids listening at home to tell their teachers to throw out the old periodic table. "Judging from the mail I later received from schoolchildren," Seaborg recalled in his autobiography, "their teachers were rather skeptical."

The Berkeley team then went on to discover berkelium (element 97) and californium (element 98) in 1949, which the *New Yorker* made fun of, as described earlier, and they kept filling in new boxes on the periodic table—keeping school-chart manufacturers in business, since they had to replace outdated charts fairly regularly. The team discovered elements 99 and 100, einsteinium and fermium, but perhaps the greatest achievement was the creation of element 101.

Because elements grow fragile as they swell with protons, scientists had difficulty creating samples large enough to spray with alpha particles. Getting enough einsteinium to even think about leapfrogging to element 101 required bombarding plutonium for three years. And that was just step one! For each attempt to create element 101, the scientists placed tiny bits of einsteinium onto gold foil and then pelted it with alpha particles. The gold then had to be dissolved away. With element 101, there weren't enough atoms to carry out any chemical reactions to confirm it had been made, so the team had to identify it in a different way—they allowed each atom of 101 to disintegrate, and then looked at the leftover pieces.

The alpha-particle step could be done in only one lab, and the detection could be done only in another a few miles away. So for each trial run, while the gold foil was dissolving, Ghiorso waited outside in his Volkswagen, motor running, to drive the sample to the other building. The team did this in the middle of the night, because the sample, if stuck in a traffic jam, might be lost and the whole effort would be wasted.

The team got the drill down, and one February night in 1955, their work paid off. In anticipation, Ghiorso had wired his radiation detector to the building's fire alarm, and when it finally detected an exploding atom of element 101, the bell rang. This happened sixteen more times that night, and with each ring, the assembled team cheered. At dawn, everyone went home tired and happy. Ghiorso forgot to unwire his detector, however, and some panic arose the next morning when a lingering atom of element 101 caused the alarm to sound one last time.

Having already honored their home city, state, and country, the Berkeley team suggested the name mendelevium, after Dmitri Mendeleev, for element 101. Scientifically, this was a no-brainer. Diplomatically, it was daring to honor a Russian scientist during the Cold War, and in the United States it was not a popular choice. Of course, the Russians loved it. Seaborg, Ghiorso, and others wanted to demonstrate that science rose above petty politics, and at the time, why not?

Seaborg would soon depart and, under Ghiorso's direction, the Berkeley lab chugged along. It practically lapped all other nuclear labs in the world, which were relegated to checking Berkeley's arithmetic.

The single time another group, from Sweden, claimed to beat Berkeley to an element, number 102, Berkeley quickly discredited the claim. Instead, Berkeley notched element 102, nobelium (after Alfred Nobel, dynamite inventor and founder of the Nobel Prizes), and element 103, lawrencium (after Berkeley Radiation Laboratory founder and director Ernest Lawrence), in the early 1960s. Meanwhile, the Russians were gearing up!

THE RUSSIANS

Some Russians have a creation myth about their corner of the planet. Way back when, the story goes, God walked the Earth, carrying all its minerals in his arms, to make sure they got distributed evenly. This plan worked well for a while. Tantalum went in one land, uranium another, and so on. But when God got to Siberia, his fingers got so cold and stiff, he dropped all the metals. His hands were too frostbitten to scoop them up, so he left them there in disgust. And this, Russians boast, explains their vast stores of minerals.

Despite those geological riches, only two useless natural elements on the periodic table were discovered in Russia, ruthenium (element 44) and samarium (element 62). Compare that poor record to the dozens of elements discovered in Sweden and Germany and France. The list of great Russian scientists beyond Mendeleev is similarly short, at least in comparison to the rest of Europe. For various reasons—including poor schools and harsh weather—Russia just never fostered the scientific genius it might have.

It didn't help when Russian leader Joseph Stalin, who came to power in 1929, started arresting scientists and forcing them to work for the state in slave labor camps. He shipped many scientists to a notorious nickel works and prison outside Norilsk, in Siberia, where temperatures regularly dropped to −80°F. Though primarily a nickel mine, Norilsk smelled permanently of sulfur (element 16), from diesel fumes, and scientists there were forced to extract a good portion of the toxic metals on the periodic table, including arsenic, lead, and cadmium (element 48). Pollution was thick in the air, and, depending on which metal was in demand, it snowed either pink or blue. When all the metals were in demand, it snowed black (and still does sometimes today). Perhaps most creepily, to this day reportedly not one tree grows within thirty miles of the poisonous nickel smelters. Much of a generation of Soviet science was wasted extracting nickel and other metals for Soviet industry.

Stalin demanded loyalty, and the Soviet nuclear-weapons program had its roots in one loyal subject, nuclear scientist Georgy Flyorov. In 1942, Flyorov noticed that despite the great progress German and American scientists had made in nuclear chemistry, scientific journals had stopped publishing on the topic. Flyorov deduced that the work had become state secrets—which could mean only one thing. In a letter that mirrored Einstein's famous letter to Franklin Roosevelt about starting the Manhattan Project,

Flyorov alerted Stalin about his suspicions. Stalin, roused and paranoid, rounded up physicists by the dozens and started them on the Soviet Union's own atomic bomb project.

Stalin and his successors were so pleased when the Soviet Union successfully tested its own nuclear bomb in 1949 that, eight years later, officials entrusted Comrade Flyorov with his own research lab. It was an isolated facility eighty miles outside Moscow, in the city of Dubna.

In Dubna, scientists reached deeper into the periodic table and tried to fuse lighter elements together. On the surface, these projects were nothing more than simple math. For element 102, you could theoretically smash magnesium into thorium (element 90) or vanadium (element 23) into gold. Few combinations stuck together, however, so scientists had to invest a lot of time in calculations to determine which pairs of elements were worth their money and effort. Flyorov and his colleagues studied hard and copied the techniques of the Berkeley lab. Seaborg, Ghiorso, and Berkeley beat the Russians to elements 101, 102, and 103. But in 1964, the Dubna team announced it had created element 104 first.

Back in the United States, anger followed shock. Its pride wounded, the Berkeley team checked the Soviet results and, not surprisingly, said they were sketchy. Meanwhile, Berkeley set out to create element 104 itself—which a Ghiorso team, advised by Seaborg, did in 1969. By that point, however, Dubna had made element 105, too. Again Berkeley scrambled to catch up, all the while saying that the Soviets were misreading their own data. Both teams produced element 106 in 1974, just months apart, and by that time all the international unity surrounding the earlier naming of mendelevium had evaporated.

Both teams began naming "their" elements. The lists of those names are too long to bother with here, but the Dubna team, perhaps inspired by Berkeley/berkelium, called one element dubnium. For its part, Berkeley named 106 seaborgium (after Glenn Seaborg)—a living person—which wasn't "illegal" but was considered tasteless in an irritatingly American way. Across the world, different element names began appearing in academic journals, and printers of the periodic table had no idea how to sort through the mess.

IUPAC

Amazingly, the argument stretched all the way into the 1990s, by which point, to add to the confusion, a team from West Germany had sprinted past the bickering Americans and Soviets to claim contested elements of their own. Eventually, the body that governs chemistry, the International Union of Pure and Applied Chemistry (IUPAC), had to step in to try to sort it all out.

In 1995, IUPAC announced official names for elements 104 to 109. The compromise pleased Dubna and Darmstadt (home of the West German group), but when the Berkeley team saw seaborgium deleted from the list, they were furious. They called a press conference to basically say, "We're using seaborgium in the U.S. of A." A powerful American chemistry group that was influential all over the world backed Berkeley up. This changed the situation, and IUPAC changed its mind. When the really final, like-it-or-not list came out in 1996, it included seaborgium at 106, as well as the official names on the table today: rutherfordium (element 104), dubnium (element 105), bohrium (element 107), hassium (element 108), and meitnerium (element 109).

But a story like this cannot end tidily. By the 1990s, the Americans were limping behind the Russians and the Germans. In remarkably quick succession, between just 1994 and 1996, the Germans discovered element 110, now named darmstadtium (Ds), after their home base; element 111, roentgenium (Rg), after the great German scientist Wilhelm Röntgen; and element 112, in June 2009, copernicium (Cn), named for Copernicus, who was the first to believe that the sun—not Earth—was the center of our solar system. Refusing to go down without a fight, in 1996 Berkeley hired a young Bulgarian named Victor Ninov—who had been part of the team that discovered elements 110 and 112.

For their big comeback, in 1999 the American team, led by Ninov's team, tried an ambitious experiment involving smashing krypton into lead to attempt to produce element 118. Many said it couldn't be done, but miraculously, the krypton experiment actually worked! "Victor must speak directly to God," scientists joked. Best of all, element 118 decayed immediately, spitting out an alpha particle and becoming element 116, which had never been seen, either. With one stroke, Berkeley had scored two elements! Rumors spread on the Berkeley campus that the team would reward old Albert Ghiorso with his own element, 118, "ghiorsium."

Except... when the Russians and Germans tried to confirm the results by rerunning the experiments, they couldn't find element 118, just krypton and lead. This made the Berkeley team rerun the experiment themselves, but they, too, found nothing, even after months of checking. When they looked back at the original data files for element 118, they noticed something sickening: There was no data! No proof element 118 existed. All signs indicated that Victor Ninov—who had controlled the all-important radiation detectors and the computer software that ran them—had made up the data. When elements exist only on computers, one person can fool the world by hijacking the technology.

Horrified, Berkeley had to withdraw its claim for 118, Ninov was fired, and the Berkeley lab suffered major budget cuts. To this day, Ninov denies that he faked any data. Even worse, American scientists were reduced to traveling to Dubna to work on heavy elements in Russia.

In 2006, an international team based in Dubna announced that after smashing ten billion billion calcium atoms into a californium target, they had produced three atoms of element 118. That claim has since been upheld, and in the past few years, three new elements named after Russian scientists and Russian cities have joined the table: flerovium (element 114), moscovium (element 115), and oganesson (element 118). But Americans can hold their heads high as well. Since the nasty battle during the Cold War, the Americans and Russians have become much more friendly, and two recent elements—made in Russia, but with the help of American scientists—have joined the table as well: livermorium (element 116), named after a government lab, and tennessine (element 117), named after Tennessee.

PART III

MISTAKES AND
RIVALRIES

CHAPTER 8

BAD CHEMISTRY

GLENN SEABORG AND ALBERT GHIORSO WERE NOT THE ONLY SCIENTISTS CHANGING the way people looked at the periodic table. Linus Pauling also helped transform periodic table chemistry. Over a few decades, starting in the 1930s, Pauling became a legend in physics and chemistry. He remains today one of the greatest scientists most people have never heard of. Although when people have heard of him, it may be for having made one of the biggest mistakes in science history.

Now, mistakes in science aren't always a bad thing. Vulcanized rubber, Teflon, and penicillin were all mistakes. Throughout history, clumsiness and outright blunders have pushed science forward, but Pauling's was not that kind of mistake—it was much bigger and much less useful. In his defense, he was working on complicated projects, but then again, he might have avoided his mistake by studying the periodic table a little more carefully.

OOPS! THAT'S NOT THE DISCOVERY I WAS TRYING TO MAKE!

FOR SCIENTISTS, MAYBE THE FAMOUS ADAGE SHOULD BE IF AT FIRST YOU DON'T SUCCEED, TRY, TRY, TRY . . . TO TURN YOUR FAILURE INTO A DIFFERENT SUCCESS. HERE ARE A FEW HAPPY ACCIDENTS YOU MIGHT BE FAMILIAR WITH:

The Slinky was invented in 1943 while mechanical engineer Richard James was trying to build a spring for ships. When he knocked some samples off a shelf, he noticed they "walked" and knew he had something special on his hands, even if it wasn't what he was initially looking for.

SLINKYS

Can you believe that Post-it Notes didn't exist before the 1970s? In 1968, Spencer Silver, an employee at technology company 3M, accidentally created an adhesive that wasn't sticky enough to use for anything. Until 1974, when a colleague of Silver's was looking for a way to mark pages in his hymnal while he sang in the church choir, he remembered Silver's seemingly useless adhesive and found a use for it!

POST-IT NOTES

During World War II, Percy LeBaron Spencer was working on how to improve a tube used in radars. One day his experiment didn't go as planned, and the candy bar in his pocket melted. He eventually tested this on corn kernels and was able to feed popcorn to his colleagues. A tasty accident!

THE MICROWAVE

OTHER ACCIDENTAL DISCOVERIES

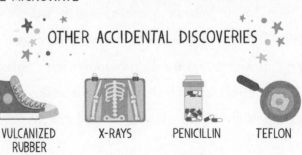

VULCANIZED RUBBER   X-RAYS   PENICILLIN   TEFLON

SHAPE MATTERS

In short, Linus Pauling figured out practically all there is to know about the chemical bonds between atoms: bond strength, bond length, bond angle, nearly everything. And since chemistry is basically the study of atoms forming and breaking bonds, Pauling single-handedly modernized chemistry.

After that triumph, Pauling continued to play with basic chemistry. He soon figured out why snowflakes are six-sided: because of the hexagonal structure of ice. At the same time, Pauling was clearly itching to move beyond simple bonds between atoms. One of his projects, for instance, determined why sickle-cell anemia kills people: the misshaped hemoglobin protein in their red blood cells cannot hold on to oxygen. This work on hemoglobin stands out as the first time anyone traced a disease to a malfunctioning molecule, and it transformed how doctors thought of medicine.

In all these cases, Pauling's real interest (besides the obvious benefits to medicine) was in how new properties emerge, almost miraculously, when small atoms automatically self-assemble into larger structures. The really fascinating thing is that larger molecules often act nothing like the atoms that they are made from. For example, sodium is a superreactive metal that burns in water. Chlorine is a poisonous green gas. Put them together and you have table salt.

Just as you could never guess, unless you'd seen it, that

individual carbon, oxygen, and nitrogen atoms could come together into something as useful as an amino acid, you'd have no idea that a few amino acids could fold themselves into all the proteins that run a living being.

This work was a step up in sophistication even from creating new elements. But that jump in sophistication also left more room for misinterpretation and mistakes. Had Pauling not blundered with a helical, spiral-shaped molecule called DNA, he would surely be considered one of the top five scientists ever.

The Shape of DNA

Like most other scientists, Pauling was not interested in DNA until 1952, even though Swiss biologist Friedrich Miescher had discovered DNA in 1869. But what was DNA? Scientists knew only a little. It came in long strands, and each strand had a phosphorus-sugar backbone. There were also nucleic bases, which stuck out from the backbone like knobs on a spine. But the shape of the strands and how they linked up were mysteries—important mysteries. As Pauling showed with hemoglobin, shape can affect how molecules work. Soon the shape of DNA became the most important question in biology.

And Pauling, like many others, assumed he was the only one smart enough to answer this question. This wasn't, or at least wasn't only, arrogance: Pauling had simply never been beaten before. So in

1952, Pauling sat down at his desk in California to crack DNA. He decided, incorrectly, that the bulky nucleic bases sat on the outside of each strand with the phosphorus-sugar backbone toward the molecule's core. Pauling also reasoned that DNA was a triple helix, with three ribbons of the phosphorus-sugar backbones forming a spiral. Unfortunately for Pauling, his data came from a dried-out DNA sample, which made the molecule seem more complicated. But on paper, all this seemed possible.

Everything was humming along nicely until Pauling asked a graduate student to check his calculations. The student did and was soon tying himself in knots trying to see where he was wrong and where Pauling was right. Eventually, the student pointed out to Pauling that something about his theory didn't seem quite right.

The graduate student explained his thinking, and Pauling, being Pauling, politely ignored him. It's not clear why Pauling bothered to have someone check his work if he wasn't going to listen, but Pauling's reason for ignoring the student is clear. He wanted scientific priority—that is, he wanted to get the credit for cracking DNA. He rushed his triple-stranded model into print in early 1953.

Meanwhile, across the Atlantic, two gawky graduate students at Cambridge University in England read Pauling's paper. Linus Pauling's son, Peter, worked in the same lab as James Watson and Francis Crick and had given the paper to them. The unknown students desperately wanted to solve DNA to make their careers. And what they read in Pauling's paper flabbergasted them: They had built the same model a year before—and had discarded it, embarrassed, when another scientist had shown that it wasn't possible.

That scientist, Rosalind Franklin, had examined wet DNA from squid and calculated that DNA had two strands of phosphorus-sugar backbones, not three. Pauling probably would have solved DNA instantly if he'd seen Franklin's good data, but in 1952, after his passport had been revoked for political reasons, he couldn't travel to an important conference in England, where he might have heard of Franklin's work.

Shaking off their disbelief, Watson and Crick rushed to their adviser (and one of Pauling's rivals), William Bragg. Bragg had won a Nobel Prize decades before but lately had become bitter about losing out on key discoveries to Pauling. Bragg had banned Watson and Crick from working on DNA after their triple-stranded embarrassment, but when they showed him Pauling's mistakes and admitted that they had continued to work in secret, Bragg saw a chance to beat Pauling. He ordered them back to DNA.

First thing, Crick wrote a cagey letter to Pauling, asking him to explain his findings. This distracted Pauling. Even while Peter Pauling alerted his father that the two students were closing in,

Pauling still insisted his three-stranded model would prove correct. Knowing that Pauling was stubborn but not stupid and would see his errors soon, Watson and Crick scrambled for ideas. They never ran experiments themselves, just brilliantly interpreted other people's data. And in 1953, they finally got the missing clue from another scientist.

That man told them that the four bases in DNA (abbreviated A, C, T, and G) always show up in paired proportions. That is, if a DNA sample is 36 percent A, it will always be 36 percent T as well. Always. The same with C and G. From this, Watson and Crick realized that A and T, and C and G, must pair up inside DNA. (Ironically, that scientist had told Pauling the same thing years before on a sea cruise. Pauling, annoyed at his vacation being interrupted by a loudmouthed colleague, had blown him off.) What's more, miracle of miracles, those two pairs of nucleic acids fit together snugly, like puzzle pieces. This explained why DNA was packed so tightly together. So while Pauling struggled with his model, Watson and Crick turned theirs inside out, making their model a sort of twisted ladder—the famed double helix. Everything checked out brilliantly, and before Pauling could recover, they published this model in the April 25, 1953, issue of *Nature*.

So how did Pauling react to the public humiliation? And to losing out—to his rival Bragg's lab, no less—on the greatest biological discovery of the century, the discovery of the blueprint of life itself?

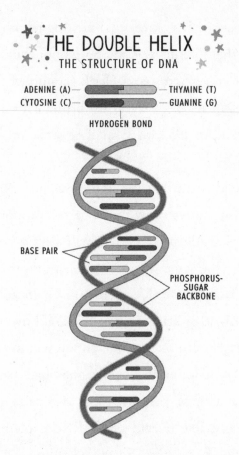

THE DOUBLE HELIX
THE STRUCTURE OF DNA

ADENINE (A) ——— ——— THYMINE (T)
CYTOSINE (C) ——— ——— GUANINE (G)

HYDROGEN BOND

BASE PAIR

PHOSPHORUS-
SUGAR
BACKBONE

With incredible dignity. The same dignity all of us should hope we could show in a similar situation. Pauling admitted his mistakes, conceded defeat, and even promoted Watson and Crick by inviting them to a professional conference he organized in late 1953.

After losing out on DNA, Pauling got a consolation prize: an overdue Nobel Prize of his own, in Chemistry, in 1954. Typical for him, Pauling then branched out into new fields. Frustrated by his chronic colds, he started experimenting on himself by taking megadoses of vitamins. For whatever reason, the doses seemed to cure him, and he excitedly told others. Eventually, his reputation as a Nobel Prize winner gave momentum to the nutritional supplement craze still going strong today, including the scientifically unlikely belief (sorry!) that vitamin C can cure a cold.

In addition, Pauling—who had refused to work on the Manhattan Project for nuclear bombs—became the world's leading anti-nuclear-weapons activist, marching in protests and writing books with titles such as *No More War!* He even won a second, surprise Nobel Prize in 1962: the Nobel Peace Prize, becoming the only person to win two unshared Nobels. He did, however, share the stage in Stockholm that year with two winners in medicine or physiology: James Watson and Francis Crick.

CHAPTER 9

POISONER'S CORRIDOR: "OUCH-OUCH"

LINUS PAULING LEARNED THE HARD WAY THAT THE RULES OF BIOLOGY ARE MUCH more delicate than the rules of chemistry. You can make changes to amino acids *chemically* and end up with basically the same molecules. However, the fragile and more complex proteins of a living creature are much more easily damaged, especially when they are contaminated with rogue elements. The most unpleasant elements can pretend to be life-giving minerals by acting like other elements that our bodies need. And the stories of how cleverly those elements damage life—the exploits of "poisoner's corridor," a cluster of deadly elements on the lower right side of the table—provide some of the darker stories of the periodic table.

Itai-Itai Disease

The lightest element in poisoner's corridor is cadmium. Miners began digging up precious metals from the Kamioka mines in Japan in AD 710. In the following centuries, the mountains of Kamioka produced gold, lead, silver (element 47), and copper (element 29), but it wasn't until twelve hundred years later that miners began to find cadmium.

The Russo-Japanese War of 1904–1905, and World War I a decade later, greatly increased Japanese demand for metals, including zinc (element 30), to use in armor, airplanes, and ammunition. Cadmium appears below zinc on the periodic table, and the two metals are often found together in nature. To purify the zinc mined in Kamioka, miners probably heated it and mixed it with acid, removing the cadmium. They then dumped the leftover cadmium sludge into streams or onto the ground, where it passed into the local water supply.

Today no one would think of dumping cadmium like that. It has become too valuable as a coating for batteries and computer parts to prevent corrosion. It also has a long history of use in pigments and leather-tanning chemicals. In the twentieth century, people even used shiny cadmium plating to line trendy drinking cups.

But the main reason no one would dump cadmium today is that it can cause terrible medical problems. Manufacturers removed cadmium from the drinking cups because hundreds of people fell ill every year when acidic fruit juices caused the cadmium to leak from the vessel walls and enter the liquids inside.

As early as 1912, doctors noticed that Japanese rice farmers near the Kamioka mines were falling ill with awful new diseases. The farmers experienced terrible joint and deep bone pain, especially the women, who made up forty-nine of every fifty cases. Their kidneys often failed, too, and their bones softened and snapped from the pressure of everyday tasks. One doctor broke a girl's wrist while taking her pulse. The mystery disease exploded in the 1930s and 1940s. As the disease passed from village to village, it became known as *itai-itai*, or "ouch-ouch," disease, after the cries of pain that came from the victims.

Only after World War II, in 1946, did a local doctor, Noboru Hagino, begin studying itai-itai disease. He first suspected malnutrition was the cause. This theory proved false, so he switched his focus to the mines. With a public health professor's help, Hagino produced a map that plotted cases of itai-itai. He made another map showing where the Jinzu River—which ran through the mines and onto the farmers' fields miles away—flowed. Laid one on top of the other, the two maps looked almost identical. After testing local crops, Hagino realized that the rice was acting as a cadmium sponge.

Zinc is an essential mineral, and just as cadmium mixes with zinc in the ground, it can also interfere with zinc in the body by replacing it. Cadmium also sometimes replaces calcium (both elements form 2+ ions), which explains why it affected people's bones. Cadmium can't perform the same roles in the body as zinc and calcium (element 20) and it cannot be flushed out of the body easily, either. The local diet depended heavily on rice, which lacks some essential nutrients, so the farmers' bodies were starved of certain minerals. Cadmium acted like those minerals so well that the farmers' cells began to weave it into their organs at even higher rates than they otherwise would have.

Hagino went public with his results in 1961. Predictably and perhaps understandably, the mining company legally responsible, Mitsui Mining and Smelting, denied all wrongdoing (it had only bought the company that had done the damage). By 1972, a national government health committee, overwhelmed by Hagino's evidence, ruled that cadmium absolutely causes itai-itai. Thirteen years later, the horror of element 48 still retained such a hold on Japan that when filmmakers needed to kill off Godzilla in the then-latest sequel, *The Return of Godzilla*, the Japanese military in the film deployed cadmium-tipped missiles. It was an atomic bomb that had given Godzilla life, so if cadmium could defeat the nuclear monster... that's a pretty dim view of this element.

Scarily, cadmium is not even the worst poison among the elements. It sits above mercury, a neurotoxin (a substance that attacks the nervous system). And to the right of mercury sit the most horrific mug shots on the periodic table—thallium (element 81), lead, and polonium (element 84)—the nucleus of poisoner's corridor.

Poisoner's Poisons

The poisoner's corridor elements are more subtle than explosive potassium (element 19) or sodium, and they can travel deep inside the body before going off. What's more, these elements (like many heavy metals on the lower right of the periodic table) can give up different numbers of electrons, depending on the circumstances. For example, potassium always loses just one electron to form K^+, but thallium can lose one or three electrons to become Tl^+ or Tl^{+3}. As a result, thallium can pretend to be many different elements and can wriggle into many different places in the body. That's why thallium is considered the deadliest element on the table.

Animal cells can be invaded by thallium. Once inside, thallium starts destroying the amino acids inside proteins, making them useless. And, unlike cadmium, thallium doesn't just stick in the bones or kidneys, but travels all over the body, and each atom can do a huge amount of damage.

For these reasons, thallium is known as the poisoner's poison. It has a gruesome record of killing many people, and the Central Intelligence Agency (the CIA) even hatched a plan to use it to kill Communist Cuba's leader, Fidel Castro. They planned to sprinkle his socks with a sort of talcum powder laced with thallium. The CIA spies were especially amused that the thallium would cause all Castro's hair, including his famous beard, to fall out. There's no record of why this plan was never attempted!

Another reason thallium, cadmium, and other related elements work so well as poisons is that they stick around for ages. I don't just mean they accumulate in the body, as cadmium does. Instead, like oxygen, these elements are likely to form stable nuclei that never go radioactive. Therefore, a fair amount of each still survives in the Earth's crust. For instance, the heaviest eternally stable element, lead, sits in box 82, a magic number.

Then there is polonium, the poisoner's poison of the nuclear age. Like thallium, it makes people's hair fall out, as the world discovered in November 2006, when Alexander Litvinenko, a former Russian spy, was poisoned by polonium in a London sushi restaurant when he drank some tea.

Past polonium (skipping over, for now, the ultrarare element astatine) sits radon. As a noble gas, radon is colorless and odorless and reacts with nothing. But as a heavy element, it displaces air, sinks into the lungs, and releases lethal radioactive particles that lead inevitably to lung cancer—just another way poisoner's corridor can get you.

Indeed, radioactivity dominates the bottom of the periodic table. Almost everything useful about heavy elements depends on how, and how quickly, they go radioactive. Probably the best way to illustrate this is through the story of a young American who grew obsessed with dangerous elements.

The Radioactive Boy Scout

David Hahn wanted to solve the world's energy crisis so badly that this Detroit sixteen-year-old, as part of an Eagle Scout project gone mad in the mid-1990s, built a nuclear reactor in a shed in his mother's backyard!

David started off small, influenced by a book called *The Golden Book of Chemistry Experiments*. He quickly outgrew a simple chemistry set and began playing with chemicals violent enough to blow his bedroom walls and carpet to bits. His mother soon sent him to the backyard shed, which suited him fine. Unfortunately, David didn't seem to get any better at chemistry. Once, before a Boy Scout meeting, he dyed his skin orange when a fake tanning chemical he was working on blew up in his face. In another accident, he exploded a container of potassium. Months later, an eye doctor was still digging pieces of plastic out of his eyes. Even after that, the disasters continued.

To get the reactor started, he wrote to government officials, pretending to be "Professor Hahn," who wanted information for his experiments. Going ridiculously far beyond the atomic energy merit badge he was originally seeking (really), David decided to build a "breeder reactor," which makes its own fuel through a clever combination of radioactive elements.

David pursued this project on weekends, since he lived with his mom only part-time after his parents' divorce. For safety's sake, he wore a dentist's lead apron to protect his organs.

Of all the work he did, probably the easiest part of the project was finding the thorium-232 that he needed for the reactor. Thorium compounds have extremely high melting points, so they glow extrabright when heated. They're too dangerous for household lightbulbs, but in mines, thorium lamps are common. Instead of wire filaments, thorium lamps use small mesh nets called mantles, and David ordered hundreds of replacement mantles from a wholesaler, no questions asked. Then he melted down the mantles into thorium ash with heat from a blowtorch. He treated the ash with $1,000 worth of lithium he had obtained by cutting open batteries with wire cutters. Heating the reactive lithium and ash over a Bunsen burner purified the thorium, giving David the thorium that he needed for his reactor core.

David then needed uranium-235. So he mounted a Geiger counter (a device that registers radioactivity with a *click–click–click–click*) on the dashboard of his Pontiac and cruised around rural Michigan, as if he'd just stumble onto a uranium hot spot in the woods. David eventually got some uranium ore from a sketchy supplier in the Czech Republic, but it was ordinary, largely useless uranium-238. Not the uranium-235 he really needed.

A few sensational media stories later said that David almost succeeded in building a reactor in the shed. In reality, he wasn't even close. He certainly gathered dangerous materials and might have shortened his life span. But that's the easy part. There are many ways to poison yourself with radioactive materials, but there are very, very few ways to get something useful from them.

Still, the police took no chances when they uncovered David's plan. They found him late one night poking around a parked car and assumed he was just a kid looking to steal tires. They searched his Pontiac, which he kindly, but stupidly, warned them was full of radioactive materials. They also found containers of strange powder and hauled him in for questioning. David was clever enough not to mention the "hot" equipment in the potting shed, most of which he'd already dismantled anyway, scared that he was making too much progress and might leave a crater.

While federal agencies tried to work out who was responsible for David—no one had tried to illegally save the world with nuclear power before—the case dragged on for months. In the meantime, David's mother, fearing her house would be condemned, slipped into the laboratory shed one night and hauled almost everything in there to the trash. Months later, officials finally stormed across the neighbors' backyards in hazmat gear to ransack the shed. Even then, the leftover cans and tools showed a thousand times more radioactivity than normal levels found in nature.

The end of the story of the radioactive Boy Scout is sad. After a few quiet years, in 2007 police caught David Hahn stealing smoke detectors from his own apartment building. With David's record, this was a significant offense, since smoke detectors run on a radioactive element, americium. Indeed, he'd already been caught once, when he was a Boy Scout, stealing smoke detectors at a summer camp.

When his mug shot was leaked to the media, David's face was pockmarked with red sores, as if he had bad acne and had picked every pimple until it bled. But thirty-one-year-old men usually don't come down with acne. The most likely explanation was that he'd been conducting more nuclear experiments. Once again, chemistry fooled David Hahn, who never realized that the periodic table is full of deception. It was an awful reminder that even though the heavy elements along the bottom of the table aren't poisonous in the usual way, they're still dangerous enough to ruin a life.

CHAPTER 10

TAKE TWO ELEMENTS, CALL ME IN THE MORNING

THE PERIODIC TABLE IS A TRICKY THING, AND MOST ELEMENTS ARE MORE COMPLICATED than the straightforward nastiness of the poisoner's corridor. An element that is toxic in one situation can become a lifesaving drug in another, and the reputations of a few element-based medicines extend back a surprisingly long time.

THE MAGIC OF SILVER

Roman officers supposedly enjoyed better health than their lowly soldiers because they ate from silver platters. Most pioneer families in early America invested in at least one good silver coin, which spent its ride across the wilderness hidden in a milk jug—not for safekeeping, but to keep the milk from spoiling. The noted gentleman astronomer Tycho Brahe, who lost his nose in a sword duel in 1564, was even said to have ordered a replacement made of silver. The metal was fashionable and, more important, prevented infections.

Archaeologists later dug up Brahe's body and found a green crust on the front of his skull—indicating that Brahe had probably worn not a silver but a cheaper, lighter copper nose. Either way, copper or silver, the story makes sense—modern science confirms that those elements have antiseptic powers. If certain microbes inch across something made of copper or silver, they absorb some of those metallic atoms. Those atoms mess up their inner workings, and the microbes die after a few hours.

The difference between silver and copper is that silver, if ingested, colors the skin blue. Permanently. Thankfully, this condition, called argyria, isn't fatal and causes no internal damage. A man in the early 1900s even made a living as "the Blue Man" in a freak show after overdosing on silver nitrate. He had taken the silver nitrate as a cure for another illness.

In more recent times, a Montana man named Stan Jones ran for the US Senate in 2002 and 2006 despite being alarmingly blue. To his credit, Jones had a good sense of humor about his condition: When asked by a reporter what he told children and adults who pointed at him on the street, he said, "I just tell them I'm practicing my Halloween costume."

Jones also gladly explained how he came to be blue. In 1995, he became obsessed with what was known as the Y2K computer crash (Y2K stood for Year 2000). The Y2K crash was expected to cause worldwide chaos, as computers that previously thought that the abbreviation "00" referred to the year 1900, would, at midnight on December 31, 1999, suddenly think that the clock had been turned back one hundred years. Some people predicted that planes would drop out of the sky and that civilization would melt down as the digital world went nuts.

Jones was especially concerned with the potential lack of antibiotics during the coming chaos. His immune system, he decided, had better get ready. So he began to brew up a silver water in his backyard. Jones drank his silver water for four and a half years, right until Y2K fizzled out in January 2000. Even though his fears didn't come to pass, Jones never regretted drinking all that silver and said he'd do it again if he ever came down with a disease. "Being alive is more important than turning purple," he said.

MIRROR IMAGES

The best modern medicines are generally not just the isolated elements that you find on the periodic table but complex compounds made from several different elements. Nevertheless, in the history of modern drugs, a few unexpected elements have played big roles. This history largely concerns lesser-known heroic scientists such as Gerhard

Domagk, but it starts with Louis Pasteur and a peculiar discovery he made about a property of molecules found in living things called handedness, which gets at the very essence of living matter.

Odds are you're right-handed, but really you're not. You're left-handed. Every amino acid that makes up every protein in your body has a left-handed twist to it. In fact, virtually every protein in every life-form that has ever existed is exclusively left-handed.

In 1849, at age twenty-six, Pasteur was asked by a winemaker to investigate tartaric acid, a harmless waste product of wine production. Grape seeds and yeast decompose into tartaric acid and collect as crystals at the bottom of wine kegs.

The tartaric acid from yeast also has a curious property. Dissolve it in water and shine a vertical slit of light through the solution, and the beam will twist clockwise, away from the vertical. It's like rotating a dial. However, human-made tartaric acid does nothing like that. A vertical beam passes through

TO UNDERSTAND THE DIFFERENCE between right-handed and left-handed molecules, look at your own hands and imagine putting a mitten on. Most mittens fit equally well on either hand, so we can say that mittens don't have a handedness. In contrast, imagine putting on a baseball glove. Baseball gloves fit on only one hand or the other, not both, so baseball gloves are right-handed or left-handed. Some molecules are the same way. And for various reasons, your body prefers molecules of one handedness over another, and molecules of the "wrong" handedness can be harmful.

the solution without being rotated. Pasteur wanted to figure out why.

He determined that it had nothing to do with the chemistry of the two types of tartaric acid. They behaved exactly the same way in chemical reactions, and exactly the same elements were present in each. Only when he examined the crystals with a magnifying glass did Pasteur notice a difference. The tartaric acid crystals from yeast all twisted in one direction, like tiny, severed left-handed fists. The human-made tartaric acid twisted both ways, a mixture of left- and right-handed fists.

Intrigued, Pasteur began the unimaginably tedious job of separating with tweezers the salt-sized grains into a lefty pile and a righty pile. He then dissolved each pile in water and tested more beams of light. Just as he suspected, the yeast crystals rotated light clockwise, while the mirror-image crystals rotated light counterclockwise, and by exactly the same number of degrees. Basically, Pasteur had shown that there are two identical but mirror-image types of tartaric acid. More important, Pasteur later expanded this idea to show that life favors molecules of only one handedness. Chemists call this left- and right-handedness "chirality."

Pasteur later admitted he'd been a little lucky with this brilliant work. Tartaric acid, unlike most molecules, is easy to see as chiral. Even more luckily, the weather cooperated. When preparing the man-made tartaric acid, Pasteur had cooled it on a windowsill. The acid separates into left- and right-handed crystals only below 79°F, and had it been warmer that season, he never would have discovered handedness. Still, Pasteur knew that luck explained just part of his success. As he himself declared, "Chance favors only the prepared mind."

You may be able to guess from his last name another contribution he made. Pasteur also developed pasteurization, a process that heats milk to kill infectious diseases. And, most famously at the time, he saved a young boy's life with his rabies vaccine. For the latter deed, he became a national hero, and he used that fame to open an institute in his name outside Paris to further his revolutionary work on germs and disease.

Not quite coincidentally, it was at the Pasteur Institute in the 1930s that scientists figured out how the first laboratory-made pharmaceuticals worked.

THE BIRTH OF ANTIBIOTICS

In early December 1935, Gerhard Domagk's young daughter, Hildegard, tripped down the staircase of the family home in Wuppertal, Germany, while holding a sewing needle. The needle punctured her hand and snapped off inside her. A doctor extracted the needle, but days later Hildegard was suffering from a high fever and a horrible infection up and down her arm. As her condition worsened, Domagk himself suffered, because death was a frighteningly common outcome for such infections. Once the bacteria began multiplying, no known drug could stop their spread.

Except there was one drug—or, rather, one possible drug. It was really a red industrial dye that Domagk had been quietly testing in his lab. On December 20, 1932, he had injected a litter of mice with ten times the lethal dose of streptococcal bacteria. He had done the same with another litter. He'd also injected the second litter with that industrial dye, Prontosil, ninety minutes later. On Christmas Eve, Domagk went back into his lab to peek. Every mouse in the second litter was alive. Every mouse in the first had died.

Germans at the time believed, a little oddly, that dyes killed germs by turning the germs' vital organs the wrong color. No one knew how they really worked, and because of that ignorance, numerous European doctors had attacked German "chemotherapy," dismissing it as inferior to surgery in treating infection.

Even Domagk didn't quite believe in his drug. The mouse experiment and the first clinical trials in humans had gone well, but with occasional serious side effects (not to mention that it caused people to flush bright red, like lobsters). Although he was willing to risk the possible deaths of patients in clinical trials for the greater good, risking his daughter was another matter.

In this dilemma, Domagk found himself in the same situation that Pasteur had been in fifty years before in France, when a young mother had brought her son, so mangled by a rabid dog he could barely walk, to Pasteur. Pasteur treated the boy with a rabies vaccine tested only on animals, and the boy lived. Pasteur wasn't a licensed doctor, and he gave the vaccine to the boy despite the threat of criminal prosecution if it failed.

If Domagk failed, he would have killed his daughter.

As Hildegard became worse and worse, he remembered the two cages of mice that Christmas Eve. When Hildegard's doctor announced that he would have to amputate her arm, Domagk decided to act. Breaking pretty much every rule in the book, he sneaked some doses of the experimental chemical from his lab and began injecting his daughter with the blood-colored drug.

At first, Hildegard worsened. Her fever alternately spiked and crashed over the next couple of weeks. But suddenly, exactly three years after her father's mouse experiment, Hildegard stabilized. She would live, with both arms intact.

Even though Domagk was obviously thrilled, he did not mention his secret experiment on Hildegard to his colleagues, only the official mouse and human trials. But his colleagues didn't need to hear about Hildegard to know that Domagk had found a blockbuster—the first genuine antibacterial drug. It's hard to overstate what a revelation this drug was. In Domagk's day, people didn't have much hope of surviving even common infections. With Prontosil, that all changed.

Despite Prontosil's success, no one really knew how it worked.

Prontosil could kill bacteria in humans and mice, but couldn't kill bacteria in a test tube. Scientists at the Pasteur Institute started investigating the structure of Prontosil in 1935 and noticed the chemical was split up into two different molecules in the body. It was actually just one of these two molecules, called sulfonamide, that killed bacteria.

Even after the discovery at the Pasteur Institute, Domagk was still rewarded with the 1939 Nobel Prize in Medicine or Physiology, just seven years after the Christmas mice experiment. But it wasn't all great. The drug Domagk had trusted to save his daughter's life became a dangerous fad. People demanded it for every sore throat and sniffle and soon saw it as some sort of cure-all. Their hopes became a horrible joke when quick-buck salesmen in the United States took advantage of this ignorance by selling the drug sweetened with antifreeze. Hundreds died within weeks.

Nevertheless, legitimate versions of this and other sulfurous chemicals have now saved millions of people's lives across the world, making Domagk's drug one of the most important discoveries in medical history.

CHAPTER 11

HOW ELEMENTS DECEIVE

EVEN AFTER HUNDREDS OF YEARS OF CHEMISTRY, ELEMENTS CONTINUE TO surprise us. It's true that chemists have a good grasp of many features of elements, such as their melting points or abundance in the Earth's crust, and on an atomic level, elements behave predictably. But when they mix with the chaos of biology, they do weird stuff. The wrong elements in the wrong place in the body can muddle up our minds and senses, and interrupt important stuff, like automatic breathing!

NASA AND NITROGEN

On March 19, 1981, five technicians working on the *Columbia* space shuttle project entered a cramped rear chamber above the engine of a simulation spacecraft at NASA's Cape Canaveral head-quarters. Seconds later, they slumped over.

Until that moment, NASA had lost no lives on the ground or in space since 1967, when three astronauts had burned to death while training for *Apollo 1*. At that time, to make spacecraft lighter, NASA allowed only pure oxygen inside spacecraft, not air, which contains 80 percent nitrogen (i.e., 80 percent deadweight). Unfortunately, as everyone (including NASA) knew, pure oxygen without nitrogen is a serious fire hazard. Some engineers worried that even static electricity from the Velcro on the astronauts' suits might ignite the pure oxygen. One day in 1967, when a spark went off without explanation during a training session, a huge fire killed the three astronauts inside the simulator.

By the 1981 *Columbia* mission, NASA had taken to filling any compartment prone to produce sparks with unreactive nitrogen (N_2). If sparks did shoot up, the nitrogen would smother them and prevent a fire. Workers who entered a nitrogen-filled compartment simply had to wear gas masks or wait until the nitrogen was pumped out and breathable air (with oxygen in it) seeped back in. On March 19, someone gave the "all clear" too soon, and the technicians crawled into the chamber unaware. Moments later they were unconscious. The nitrogen not only prevented their heart cells from absorbing new oxygen but also stole the little oxygen that cells stored up for hard times. Three men were saved but, sadly, two died.

TRICKING THE SENSES

Besides our respiratory system, which controls breathing, our bodies also have sensory equipment, which allows us to touch and taste and smell. We trust our senses for true information about the world and for protection from danger, and it can be a little frightening to learn how easily our senses can be tricked.

Alarm receptors inside your mouth will tell you to drop a spoonful of soup before it burns your tongue, but, oddly, chili peppers contain a chemical, capsaicin, that irritates those receptors, too. Peppermint cools your mouth because minty menthol seizes up cold receptors, leaving you shivering as if an arctic blast had just blown through.

Elements pull similar tricks with smell and taste. If someone spills the tiniest bit of tellurium (element 52) on himself, he will reek like pungent garlic for weeks, and for hours after he's been in a room, people will know he was there. Even more baffling, beryllium (element 4) tastes like sugar. More than any other nutrient, humans need quick energy from sugar to live, and after thousands of years of hunting for food in the wild, you'd think we'd have pretty sophisticated equipment to detect sugar. Yet beryllium—a pale, hard-to-melt, insoluble metal with small atoms that look nothing like sugar molecules—lights up taste buds the same way sugar does.

This disguise might be simply amusing, except that beryllium, though sweet in small doses, becomes toxic very quickly. Some people are affected by something called acute beryllium disease, the periodic table equivalent of a peanut allergy. Even for the rest of us, exposure to beryllium powder can scar the lungs.

Beryllium can trick people in part because humans have such a screwy sense of taste. Now, some of the five types of taste buds are reliable. The taste buds for bitterness examine food, especially plants, for poisonous nitrogen chemicals, such as the cyanide in apple seeds. The taste buds for savory lock onto glutamate, the G in MSG. Glutamate helps to build proteins, so these taste buds alert you to protein-rich foods.

But the taste buds for sweet and sour are easy to confuse. Beryllium tricks them, as does a special protein in the berries of some species of plants. Named miraculin, this protein strips out the unpleasant sourness in foods without changing the other parts of their tastes, so that apple cider vinegar tastes like apple cider (without the sharp vinegar taste), or Tabasco tastes like regular tomato sauce (without the spicy burn). On a molecular level, "sour" is simply what we taste when our taste buds open up and charged hydrogen ions (H^+) in acids rush in.

The taste buds for salty also are affected by the flow of charges, but only the charges on certain elements. Sodium tastes salty to our tongues most strongly, but potassium, sodium's chemical cousin, tastes salty, too. Both elements exist as charged ions (Na^+ and K^+) in nature, and it's mostly that charge, not the sodium or potassium, that the tongue detects.

Of course, taste being so complicated, saltiness isn't as tidy as that last paragraph may suggest. We also taste useless ions that act like sodium and potassium as salty (e.g., lithium and ammonium). And, depending on what sodium and potassium are paired with, they can taste even sweet or sour. Sometimes, as with potassium chloride, the same molecules taste bitter at low concentrations but taste very salty at high concentrations. Potassium can also shut the tongue down. Chewing raw potassium gymnemate, a chemical in the leaves of the plant *Gymnema sylvestre*, will make piles of raw sugar heaped on the tongue taste like sand.

TASTE TESTS

You can do your own taste experiments at home. Look in your cupboards and refrigerator for foods that represent all five taste buds: sweet, sour, savory, salty, and bitter, and record your findings.

All this suggests that taste is a really bad guide to sorting the elements. And however good our brains may be at sorting through chemical information in a lab or designing chemistry experiments, our senses will do their own thing and find garlic in tellurium and powdered sugar in beryllium. When it comes to the periodic table, it's probably best to keep our mouths shut!

TROUBLE WITH IODINE

A live body is so complicated that there's almost no telling what will happen if you inject a random element into your bloodstream or liver. Even the brain can be affected. Our logic, wisdom, and judgment can also be confused by elements such as iodine (element 53).

Perhaps this shouldn't be a surprise, since iodine has been deceptive since its beginning. Elements tend to get increasingly heavy from left to right across the rows of the periodic table, and in the 1860s, Dmitri Mendeleev said that increasing atomic weight was a universal law of matter. The problem is that universal laws of nature cannot have exceptions, and Mendeleev knew of an exception in the bottom right-hand corner of the table. In order for tellurium and iodine to line up beneath similar elements on the table (as they should), tellurium must fall to the left of iodine. However, tellurium outweighs iodine, and it kept stubbornly outweighing it no matter how many times chemists reweighed it. Facts is facts.

Scientists know of four pair reversals among the ninety-two natural elements today—argon-potassium, cobalt-nickel, iodine-tellurium, and thorium-protactinium—as well as a few among the ultraheavy, human-made elements. But a century after Mendeleev, iodine got caught up in a much larger deception. You see, a rumor persists to this day among the billion people in India that Mohandas K. Gandhi, that greatest of all Indian leaders, absolutely hated iodine.

In 1930, Gandhi led the Indian people in the famous Salt March to Dandi, to protest the crazy British salt tax. Salt was one of the few things such a poor country could produce on its own. Indian people simply gathered seawater, let it evaporate, and sold the dry salt on the street. The British government's taxing of salt production at 8.2 percent was like charging Eskimos for making ice.

To protest this, Gandhi and seventy-eight followers left for a 240-mile march on March 12. They picked up more and more people at each village, and by the time they arrived in the coastal town of Dandi on April 6, they formed a train two miles long. Gandhi gathered his followers for a rally, and at its climax he scooped up a handful of salty mud and cried, "With this, I am shaking the foundation of the [British] Empire!" He encouraged everyone to make illegal, untaxed salt, and by the time India gained independence seventeen years later, so-called common salt was indeed common in India.

The only problem was that common salt contains very little iodine, an ingredient crucial to health. By the early 1900s, Western countries had figured out that adding iodine to the diet is the cheapest and most effective health measure a government can take to prevent birth defects and mental illness. Following Switzerland in 1922, many countries made it the law to include iodine in salt, since salt is a cheap, easy way to deliver the helpful element. Indian doctors soon realized that they could save millions of children by putting iodine in their salt, too.

But even many years after Gandhi's march to Dandi, salt was still being produced the old-fashioned way, and salt that contained iodine was still not popular. As the health benefits became clearer, and as India modernized, some Indian state governments banned common salt between the 1950s and 1990s. In 1998, when the Indian federal government forced three remaining Indian states to ban common salt, there was a backlash.

Mom-and-pop salt makers protested about the added processing costs. Some people even worried, without any evidence, that salt with iodine would spread cancer, diabetes, and tuberculosis. These opponents worked frantically, and just two years later—with the United Nations and every doctor in India horrified—the Indian prime minister reversed the federal ban on common salt. The consumption of salt with iodine fell 13 percent nationwide. Birth defects went up.

Luckily, the reversal lasted only until 2005, when a new Indian prime minister again banned common salt. But this has not solved India's iodine problem. Gandhi's misunderstood influence in the argument makes older Indians distrusting. And although it would cost India just a penny per person per year to produce enough salt with iodine for its citizens, the costs of transporting salt are high, and half the country—half a billion people—still cannot get salt with iodine on a regular basis.

PART IV

THE ELEMENTS OF
HUMAN CHARACTER

CHAPTER 12

POLITICAL ELEMENTS

THE PERIODIC TABLE REFLECTS OUR FRUSTRATIONS AND FAILURES IN EVERY HUMAN field: economics, psychology, the arts, and—as Gandhi and the story of iodine prove—politics. As well as a scientific one, there's a social history of the elements, too. That history can best be traced through Europe, starting in the country that we now know as Poland.

POLISH POLITICS

Poland did not exist when one of the most famous Poles ever, Marie Skłodowska, was born in Warsaw in 1867, at the same time Mendeleev was constructing his great tables. Four years earlier, the Russians had taken control of Warsaw, after the Polish people attempted to gain independence. Russia had backward views on educating women, so the girl's father tutored her himself. She was particularly interested in (and good at) science, but she also joined some political groups that wanted independence for Poland.

After demonstrating too often against the wrong people, Skłodowska had to move to Poland's other great cultural center, Kraków. Even there, she could not get the scientific training she wanted. She finally moved to the Sorbonne in faraway Paris. She planned to return to her homeland after she earned a PhD, but, having fallen in love with Pierre Curie, she decided to stay in France.

In the 1890s, Marie and Pierre Curie began perhaps the most fruitful partnership in science history. Studying radioactive elements—those with unstable nuclei—was the new field of the day, and Marie's work on uranium, the heaviest natural element, was brilliant. The Curies shared the 1903 Nobel Prize in Physics for their work with radioactivity and uranium.

Throughout the time that she was in France, Marie never stopped viewing herself as Polish. Indeed, Curie was an early example of a species whose population exploded during the twentieth century—the refugee scientist. Science, like any other human activity, has always been filled with politics, and the twentieth century is full of examples of politics and empires warping science. Scientists often buried their heads in lab work and hoped that the world around them would figure out its problems as neatly as their equations—a mistake.

Not long after winning the Nobel Prize, Curie made another discovery. After performing experiments to purify uranium, she noticed that the leftover "waste" (which she normally had simply threw away) was three hundred times more radioactive than uranium.

Hopeful that the waste contained an unknown element, she and her husband began boiling down thousands of pounds of pitchblende, a uranium ore, in a cauldron and stirring it with "an iron rod almost as big as myself," she later said. It took years of tedious work, and all they got was a few grams of the residue

OTHER REFUGEE SCIENTISTS

Albert Einstein: You know who he is, but did you know he was a German Jew who was among several scholars who had to flee to America? He arrived in 1933 and helped start an organization to assist other refugees arriving from Europe.

Enrico Fermi: The Italian physicist left Italy in 1938 to protect his Jewish wife and emigrated to the United States, where he joined the Manhattan Project. He was one of many refugee scientists on the team that created the atomic bomb.

Lise Meitner: An Austrian Jew who escaped the Nazis by fleeing to Sweden, she was instrumental in the race to create a nuclear bomb (although, like many of the scientists involved, later regretted her contribution to the weapon).

to study. But from those few grams, they discovered *two* new elements. In 1911, she won another Nobel Prize, this time in Chemistry.

As discoverers of the new elements, the Curies earned the right to name them, and Marie called the first element they isolated polonium—from Polonia, the Latin for Poland—after her home-land. No element had been named for a political cause before, and Marie hoped that her choice would help the Polish struggle for independence.

But naming her first element after Poland contributed nothing. Worse, the second element she discovered, radium (element 88), glowed an amazing green color and soon appeared in consumer products worldwide. People even drank water with radium added, from radium-lined ceramic jugs called Revigators, as a health tonic.

Overall, radium overshadowed polonium and caused exactly the sensation that Curie had hoped for with the element named after Poland. Even worse, polonium was linked to lung cancer from cigarettes, since tobacco plants absorbed polonium excessively well and concentrated it in their leaves.

Irène Joliot-Curie, Marie's daughter, also suffered at the hands of polonium. A brilliant scientist herself, Irène and her husband, Frédéric Joliot-Curie, picked up on Marie's work, and Irène won her own Nobel Prize in 1935. Unfortunately, one day in 1946, a capsule of polonium exploded in Irène's laboratory, and she inhaled Marie's beloved element. Joliot-Curie died of leukemia in 1956, just as her mother had twenty-two years before.

Ironically, radioactive substances have since become crucial medical tools. When swallowed in small amounts, radioactive "tracers" light up organs and soft tissue just as X-rays show bones.

Virtually every hospital in the world uses tracers, and a whole branch of medicine called radiology deals with them.

LEFTOVERS AND TRACERS

In 1910, just before Marie Curie collected her second Nobel Prize for radioactivity, young György Hevesy arrived in England to study radioactivity himself. His university's lab director in Manchester, Ernest Rutherford, immediately assigned Hevesy the Herculean task of separating out radioactive atoms from non-radioactive atoms inside blocks of lead. Actually, it turned out to be not Herculean but impossible. Rutherford had assumed the radioactive atoms, known as radium-D, were a unique substance. In fact, radium-D was radioactive lead and therefore could not be separated chemically. Ignorant of this, Hevesy wasted two years tediously trying to tease lead and radium-D apart before giving up.

Hevesy—a bald, droopy-cheeked, mustached aristocrat from

> **DOUBLE NOBEL**
>
> Not only was Marie Curie part of the only mother-daughter pair to win the prize (six father-son duos have won it), but she was also the first scientist ever to win the Nobel Prize twice. In 1903, she was awarded the prize in Physics, and in 1911, she was awarded in Chemistry. Only three others have double-medaled:
>
> **Linus Pauling**: 1954 (Chemistry), 1962 (Peace)
>
> **Frederick Sanger**: 1958, 1970 (both in Chemistry)
>
> **John Bardeen**: 1956, 1972 (both in Physics)

Hungary—also faced domestic frustrations. Hevesy was far from home and used to savory Hungarian food, not the English cooking at his boardinghouse. After noticing patterns in the meals served there, Hevesy grew suspicious that, like a high school cafeteria recycling Monday's hamburgers into Thursday's beef chili, his landlady's "fresh" daily meat was anything but. When confronted, she denied this, so Hevesy decided to seek proof.

Miraculously, he'd achieved a breakthrough in the lab around that time. He still couldn't separate radium-D, but he realized he could flip that to his advantage. He'd begun musing over the possibility of injecting minute quantities of dissolved lead into a living creature and then tracing the element's path, since the creature would metabolize the radioactive and nonradioactive lead the same way, and the radium-D would emit beacons of radioactivity as it moved. If this worked, he could actually track molecules inside veins and organs, an unprecedented degree of resolution.

Before he tried this on a living being, Hevesy decided to test his idea on the tissue of a nonliving being, a test with an ulterior motive. He took too much meat at dinner one night and, when the landlady's back was turned, sprinkled "hot" lead over it. She gathered his leftovers as normal, and the next day Hevesy brought home a newfangled radiation detector from his lab buddy, Hans Geiger. Sure enough, when he waved it over that night's goulash, Geiger's counter went furious: *click-click-click-click*. Hevesy confronted his landlady with the evidence. But, being a scientific romantic, Hevesy no doubt laid it on thick as he explained the mysteries of radioactivity. In fact, the landlady was so charmed to be caught so cleverly, with the latest tools of forensic science, she didn't even get mad. There's no historical record of whether she altered her menu, however.

CHEMISTRY VERSUS PHYSICS

In the 1920s, chemistry and physics were battling with each other, and most scientists picked sides. And at that time Niels Bohr (a famous physicist) unwittingly opened the crack between chemistry and physics into a real political rift.

In 1922, the box for element 72 on the periodic table was blank. Chemists had figured out that the elements between 57 (lanthanum) and 71 (lutetium) were all rare earths, but nobody was sure about element 72.

According to the story, Niels Bohr in Copenhagen came up with a plan for hunting the element, based on the new science of quantum mechanics. The key point, said Bohr, was that element 72 was *not* a rare earth but a proper transition metal. Bohr therefore asked Hevesy (who had moved to Copenhagen after his tracers discovery helped his career blossom) and physicist Dirk Coster to look at samples of zirconium (element 40)—the element above number 72 on the table and probably its closest chemical relation. In perhaps the easiest discovery in periodic table history, Hevesy and Coster found element 72 on their first attempt. They named it hafnium, from Hafnia, the Latin name for Copenhagen.

That's the story anyway, but the truth is a little different. At least three scientists before Bohr wrote papers dating as far back as 1895 that linked element 72 to transition metals such as zirconium. It seemed that Bohr had poached their arguments.

Yet, as with most legends, what's important isn't necessarily the truth but rather how people react to a story. People clearly wanted to believe that Bohr had found hafnium through quantum mechanics (i.e., physics) alone and not through chemistry. Some people even proclaimed that Mendeleevian chemistry was dead and Bohrian physics ruled. What started as a scientific argument became a political dispute about territory and boundaries. Such is science, such is life.

Colleagues had already nominated Hevesy for a Nobel Prize by 1924 for discovering hafnium, but there was a dispute with Georges Urbain—a French chemist—over who had found hafnium first. Most scientists didn't find Urbain's work convincing, and in 1924, Europe was still divided by World War I. The dispute became the French versus Bohr and Hevesy, who were considered Germans by the French, even though they were Danish and Hungarian, respectively. Chemists also mistrusted Hevesy for his dual "citizenship" in chemistry and physics, and that, along with the political bickering, prevented the Nobel committee from giving him the prize. Instead, it left the 1924 prize blank.

Despite the injustice, Hevesy continued to work with others, including Irène Joliot-Curie. In fact, Hevesy was a witness to an enormous mistake by Joliot-Curie, one that prevented her from making one of the great scientific discoveries of the twentieth century. That honor fell to another woman, an Austrian Jew, who, like Hevesy, left Germany to get away from the Nazis. Unfortunately, Lise Meitner's run-in with politics, both worldly and scientific, ended rather worse than Hevesy's.

CREDIT WHERE IT'S DUE

Meitner and Otto Hahn began working together in Germany just before the discovery of element 91. Its discoverer, Polish chemist Kazimierz Fajans, had found only very short-lived atoms of the element in 1913, so he named it brevium, meaning "brief." Meitner and Hahn realized that most atoms of element 91 actually hung around for hundreds of thousands of years, which made "brevium" sound a little stupid. They renamed it protactinium, or "parent of actinium," the element it (eventually) turned into. No doubt Fajans protested this rejection of his name, but regardless, "brevium" lost out, "protactinium" stuck, and Meitner and Hahn sometimes receive credit for codiscovering element 91 today.

However, that's not quite the end of the story of protactinium. Meitner and Hahn continued to work closely together: He performed the chemistry, identifying what elements were present in radioactive samples, and she performed the physics, figuring out how Hahn had gotten what he said. Unusually, though, Meitner performed *all* the work for the final protactinium experiments because Hahn was distracted with research for Germany's gas warfare during World War I. She nevertheless made sure he received credit. (Remember that favor.)

After the war, they resumed their partnership, but while the decades between the wars were thrilling in Germany scientifically, they proved scary politically. Hahn—strong-jawed, mustached, of good German stock—had nothing to fear from the Nazi takeover in 1933. Yet, to his credit, when Hitler quickly ran all the Jewish scientists out of the country, Hahn resigned his professorship in protest. For her part, even though she had Jewish grandparents, Meitner downplayed the danger and buried herself in scintillating new discoveries in nuclear physics.

The biggest of those discoveries came in 1934, when Enrico Fermi announced that by pelting uranium atoms with atomic particles, he had created the first artificial elements heavier than uranium. This wasn't true, but people were so excited by the idea that the periodic table was no longer limited to just ninety-two elements that new ideas about nuclear physics kept scientists around the world busy.

That same year, Irène Joliot-Curie did similar experiments. After careful chemical analysis, she announced that the new heavy elements were similar to lanthanum, the first rare earth. This was unexpected—so unexpected that Hahn didn't believe it. He politely told Frédéric Joliot-Curie that the lanthanum link was hogwash and that he would redo Irène's experiments to prove it.

Also in 1938, because of her Jewish roots, Meitner was forced to leave Germany. She found refuge in Sweden. Hahn remained faithful to Meitner, and the two continued to write to each other and even met occasionally in Copenhagen. During one such meeting in late 1938, Hahn arrived a little shaken. After repeating Irène Joliot-Curie's experiments, he had found her elements. And they not only behaved *like* lanthanum (and another nearby element she'd found, barium) but, according to every known chemical test, they *were* lanthanum and barium (element 56). He was confused.

Meitner wasn't confused. She alone (after discussions with her nephew and new partner, physicist Otto Frisch) realized that Fermi hadn't discovered new elements; he'd discovered nuclear fission. He'd split uranium into smaller elements and misunderstood his results. The eka-lanthanum Joliot-Curie had found was nothing more than plain lanthanum. Hevesy realized that Joliot-Curie had been so close to making that unimaginable discovery. But Joliot-Curie, Hevesy said, "didn't trust herself enough" to believe what she had seen. Meitner trusted herself, and she convinced Hahn that everyone else was wrong.

Naturally, Hahn wanted to publish these amazing results, but his connection to Meitner made doing so politically tricky. They discussed options, and Meitner agreed to name just Hahn and his assistant on the key paper. Meitner and Frisch's contributions, which made sense of everything, appeared later in a separate journal.

The Nobel committee had decided by 1943 to reward nuclear fission with a prize. The question was, who deserved it? Hahn, clearly. But the war had isolated Sweden and made it impossible to interview scientists about Meitner's contributions, an important part of the committee's decision. The committee therefore relied on scientific journals—which arrived months late or not at all, and many of which, especially the German ones, had left Meitner out of the discussion altogether. Also, the divisions between chemistry and physics made it hard to reward work that combined the two sciences.

Hahn's supporters pointed out that Meitner had done no work "of great importance" in the previous few years—hardly surprising, since at the time she was hiding from Hitler. Meitner's biggest supporter on the Nobel committee argued for a shared prize and probably would have gotten what he wanted, but when he died unexpectedly, Hahn was awarded the 1944 prize alone.

Shamefully, when Hahn got word of his win, he didn't speak up for Meitner. As a result, Meitner got nothing, largely because of politics.

The committee could have made up for this horrible oversight in 1946 or later, after the historical record made Meitner's contributions clear. But the Nobel committee is not enthusiastic about admitting mistakes. Despite being repeatedly nominated her whole life, Meitner died in 1968 without her Nobel Prize.

Happily, history has a funny way of correcting such things. Element 105 was originally named hahnium, after Otto Hahn, by Glenn Seaborg, Albert Ghiorso, and others in 1970. But during the dispute over naming rights, an international committee stripped the element of that name in 1997, calling it dubnium instead. Because of the odd rules for naming elements—basically, each name gets one shot—hahnium can never be considered as the name for a new element in the future, either, so the Nobel Prize is all Hahn got. However, Meitner soon got a far more exclusive honor than a prize given out yearly. Element 109 is now, and forever will be, known as meitnerium.

CHAPTER 13

ELEMENTS AS MONEY

IF THE PERIODIC TABLE HAS A HISTORY WITH POLITICS, THEN IT HAS AN EVEN LONGER and even closer relationship with money. The stories of many metallic elements cannot be told without getting tangled up in the history of money, which also means getting tangled up in the history of counterfeiting—the faking of money.

In different centuries, cattle, spices, porpoise teeth, salt, cocoa beans, cigarettes, beetle legs, and tulips have all been used as money, none of which can be faked convincingly or easily. It's tough to make a fake cow! Metals are much easier to counterfeit. Transition metals are especially easy, since they have similar chemistries and densities (because they have similar electron structures) and they can blend together and replace one another in mixtures of metals known as alloys.

MIDAS'S ZINC TOUCH

Around 700 BC, a prince named Midas inherited the kingdom of Phrygia in what is now Turkey. Midas sometimes receives credit for discovering tin (not true, though it *was* mined in his kingdom) and for discovering some other minerals, but no one would remember Midas today if not for his infamous golden touch. He earned it after helping the minor Greek god Silenus, who passed out in his rose garden one night. Silenus so appreciated the monarch's hospitality that he offered Midas a reward. Midas asked that whatever he touched transform into gold—a delight that soon cost him his daughter when he hugged her, and almost cost him his life, since for a time even food turned into gold when it touched his lips.

Obviously, none of that probably ever happened to the real king. But there's evidence that Midas earned his legendary status for good reason. It all traces back to the Bronze Age, which began in Midas's neighborhood around 3000 BC. Making bronze, an alloy of tin and copper, was the high-tech field of the day. But in saying "bronze," we need to be more specific. It's not like water, in which two parts hydrogen always combine with one part oxygen. Many different mixtures with many different ratios of metals all count as bronze, and around the ancient world, bronze metals varied in color, depending on the different percentages of tin, copper, and other elements that were present.

One unique feature of the metal mines near Phrygia was that they contained many ores with zinc. Zinc and tin are commonly found together in nature, and it is easy to mistake one metal for the other. What's interesting is that zinc mixed with copper doesn't form bronze; it forms brass. And the earliest known brass foundries were found where Midas once reigned.

Is it obvious yet? Go find something bronze and then something brass, and examine them. The bronze is shiny, but with a reddish copper color. You wouldn't mistake it for anything else. The color of brass is much more golden. Midas's touch was possibly nothing more than an accidental "touch" of zinc in the soil of his kingdom. Greek travelers probably loved the Phrygian "bronzes" because they were so much brighter than their own. The tales they sent home might have grown, century by century, until golden-colored brass became real gold, and Midas's legendary superpower to create precious metals at a touch became the story. A myth with a believable origin.

COUNTERFEIT CURRENCY

Midas's zinc is a case of unintentional deception: an innocent moment in history that is surrounded by many other examples of deliberate counterfeiting. A century after Midas, the first real money appeared in Asia, coins made of a natural silver-gold alloy called electrum. Then another fabulously wealthy ancient ruler, King Croesus, figured out how to separate electrum into silver and gold coins, and in the process established a real currency system. Just a few years later, in 540 BC, King Polycrates, on the Greek isle Samos, began buying off his enemies in Sparta with worthless lead that had been plated on the outside with gold. Ever since then, counterfeiters have used elements such as lead, copper, tin, and iron to make the real money stretch a little further.

If the chemistry of metal coins once favored the cheats, in the age of paper money, the unique chemistry of metals such as europium (element 63) helps governments prevent counterfeiting. It all traces back to the chemistry of europium and especially the movement of electrons within its atoms.

So far we've discussed only the movement of electrons between atoms, but electrons constantly whirl around their own nuclei, too, a lot like planets circling a sun. But electrons cannot take just any old path around a nucleus. They move in very specific paths, each having its own specific energy. There's no energy level between the first path and the second path, nor is there any energy level between the second path and the third path, and so on. That means electrons are allowed to orbit only at certain, very specific distances from their "sun." They whiz around in weird shapes and at funny angles but always at fixed distances from the nucleus.

However, if an electron is given a burst of energy by heat or the shining of light, then it can jump from a low-energy path to an empty, higher-energy path. Unfortunately, the electron cannot stay in the high-energy state for long and soon crashes back down. As the electron crashes down, it releases the energy that it gained when it jumped up by giving out light.

The color of the light that the electron releases depends on the relative energies of the starting and ending levels. A crash between closely spaced levels releases low-energy reddish light, while a crash between more widely spaced levels releases high-energy violet light. The light given off by electrons in atoms in this way is always made up of very specific, very pure colors. Each element's shells sit at different energies, so each element releases its own, characteristic bands of color that are unique to it—the very bands Robert Bunsen observed with his burner and spectroscope.

HOW ENERGY CHANGES AN ELECTRON'S BEHAVIOR

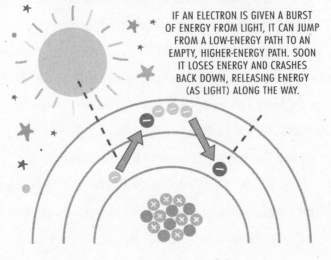

IF AN ELECTRON IS GIVEN A BURST OF ENERGY FROM LIGHT, IT CAN JUMP FROM A LOW-ENERGY PATH TO AN EMPTY, HIGHER-ENERGY PATH. SOON IT LOSES ENERGY AND CRASHES BACK DOWN, RELEASING ENERGY (AS LIGHT) ALONG THE WAY.

Europium can give out light as described above, but not very well. Europium and other lanthanides can emit light in a different way, called fluorescence. Fluorescence involves whole molecules rather than just electrons. Fluorescent molecules absorb high-energy light (ultraviolet light) but emit that energy as lower-energy, visible light. Depending on the molecule it's attached to, europium can emit red, green, or blue light.

The European Union (EU) uses europium in the ink on its paper bills (a nice coincidence!). To prepare the ink, EU treasury chemists put europium ions in the fluorescing dye. The europium appears dull under visible light, and a counterfeiter may think that he has a perfect replica. But beneath a special laser, the sketch of Europe glows green. Stars become yellow or red, and monuments and signatures and hidden seals shine royal blue. Officials can spot counterfeits simply by looking for bills that don't show all these signs.

There are really two euros on each banknote, then: the one we see day to day and a second, hidden euro mapped directly onto the first—an embedded code. This effect is extremely hard to fake without professional training. The europium dyes make the euro the most sophisticated piece of currency ever devised. Europium-dyed banknotes certainly haven't stopped counterfeiting; that's probably impossible as long as people like holding cash. But in the periodic table–wide struggle to slow it down, europium has taken a place among the most precious metals.

From Precious to Productive

Ounce by ounce, the most valuable element, among the elements you can actually buy, is rhodium (element 45). (That's why, to trump a mere platinum record, the *Guinness Book of Records* gave former Beatle Paul McCartney a disc made of rhodium in 1979 to celebrate his becoming the bestselling musician of all time.) But no one ever made more money more quickly with an element on the periodic table than the American chemist Charles Hall did with aluminium (element 13).

Because of its shininess, aluminium was once classified as a precious metal, like silver or platinum (element 78), worth hundreds of dollars an ounce. In the mid-1800s, a Frenchman figured out how to extract the metal for industry, making aluminium available commercially. For a price. It was still more expensive than even gold. That's because, despite being the most common metal in the Earth's crust—around 8 percent of it by weight, hundreds of millions of times more common than gold—aluminium never appears in its pure form. It's always bonded to something else, usually oxygen. Pure samples were considered miracles.

The French once displayed aluminium bars next to their crown jewels, and Emperor Napoleon III reserved a prized set of aluminium cutlery for special guests at banquets. (Less-favored guests used gold knives and forks.) In the United States, government engineers, to show off their country's industrial achievements, capped the

Washington Monument with a six-pound pyramid of aluminium in 1884.

Aluminium's sixty-year reign as the world's most precious metal was glorious, but soon an American chemist ruined everything. The metal's properties—light, strong, attractive—and the fact that there is so much of it in the Earth's crust, had people pretty excited. But no one could figure out an easy way to separate it from oxygen. That was until a student at Oberlin College in Ohio named Charles Hall solved the problem.

Hall worked on separating aluminium throughout his undergraduate years at Oberlin. He failed and failed and failed again, but failed a little more smartly each time. Finally, in 1886, Hall ran an electric current from handmade batteries (power lines didn't exist) through a liquid with dissolved aluminium compounds. The energy from the current separated the pure metal from the oxygen, which collected as tiny silver-colored nuggets on the bottom of the tank. The process was cheap and easy, and it would work just as well in huge vats as it had on the lab bench. This had been the most sought-after chemical prize for years, and Hall had found it. The "aluminium boy wonder" was just twenty-three.

Hall's fortune was not made instantly. Another chemist, Paul Héroult in France, stumbled on more or less the same process at the same time. (Today, Hall and Héroult share credit for the discovery.) An Austrian invented another separation method in 1887, and with the competition heating up, Hall quickly founded what became the Aluminum Company of America, or Alcoa, in Pittsburgh. It turned into one of the most successful business ventures in history.

Aluminium production at Alcoa grew incredibly quickly. In its first months in 1888, Alcoa made 50 pounds of aluminium per day; two decades later, it produced 88,000 pounds per day to meet the demand. And while production went up, prices went down— dramatically. Years before Hall was born, one man's breakthrough had dropped aluminium from $550 per pound to $18 per pound in seven years. Fifty years later, Hall's company drove down the price to 25 cents per pound. At his death in 1914, Hall owned Alcoa shares worth $30 million (around $650 million today).

And thanks to Hall, aluminium became the utterly super-common metal we all know today; the basis for pop cans and pinging Little League bats and airplane bodies. I suppose it depends on your taste whether you think aluminium was better off as the world's most precious or most productive metal.

Incidentally, throughout this book I use the international spelling "aluminium" instead of the strictly American "aluminum." This spelling disagreement traces its roots back to the early 1800s. The original spelling matched the "ium" of the recently discovered barium, magnesium, sodium, and strontium (element 38). When Charles Hall applied for patents on his electric-current process, he used the extra *i*, too. However, when advertising his shiny metal, Hall was looser with his language. There's debate about whether cutting the *i* was intentional or simply a mistake on the advertisements, but when Hall saw "aluminum," he thought it brilliant, since it aligned his product with the very classy platinum. His new metal caught on so quickly and grew so economically important that "aluminum" became the American spelling. As always in the United States, money talks.

CHAPTER 14

ARTISTIC ELEMENTS

AS SCIENCE GREW MORE SOPHISTICATED THROUGHOUT ITS HISTORY, IT ALSO grew more expensive, and big money began to decide if, when, and how, science got done.

Of course, during the eighteenth and nineteenth centuries, very few people, mostly rich gentlemen, could afford a little workshop in which to do their science. It's no coincidence that people from the upper classes were usually the ones discovering new elements: No one else had the time or the money to sit around and argue about what some mysterious rocks were made of.

These well-to-do gentlemen throughout Europe received educations heavy in the classics (Greek and Latin), and many element names—cerium, thorium, promethium—point to ancient myths. The really funny-looking names, too, such as praseodymium (element 59), molybdenum (element 42), and dysprosium (element 66), are mixtures of Latin and Greek. Dysprosium means "little hidden one," since it's tricky to separate from its brother elements. Praseodymium means "green twin" for similar reasons (its other half is neodymium, or "new twin"). The names of noble gases mostly mean "stranger" or "inactive."

All this seems odd today—scientists receiving more training in Latin and Greek than, well, in science—but for centuries science was less a profession than a hobby for amateurs. Science didn't rely much on mathematics back then, and it was easy for anyone to say they were a scientist. Any nobleman, even one without much scientific or math training, could bully his way into scientific discussions, qualified or not.

One such nobleman was a famous German writer, Johann Wolfgang von Goethe—probably best known in America for writing the play *Faust*. Many people still rank him as the greatest, most accomplished German ever to live. Goethe's theories relied as much on poetry as science, but he did make one lasting contribution to science generally—and to the periodic table.

DÖBEREINER'S TRIADS

In 1809, as a minister of the state, Goethe had the responsibility of picking a scientist for an open position in the chemistry department at the University of Jena. After hearing recommendations from friends, Goethe had the foresight to select another Johann Wolfgang—J. W. Döbereiner.

Döbereiner's greatest contribution to science was inspired by one of the rare elements, strontium. A couple doctors discovered strontium in a hospital lab in 1790. They named it after the origin of the minerals they were studying—Strontian, a mining village in Scotland—and Döbereiner picked up his work twenty years later. Döbereiner's research focused on finding precise ways to weigh elements, and strontium was new and rare, a challenge. With Goethe's encouragement, he set out to study the characteristics of the new metal.

As he refined his figures on strontium, though, he noticed something odd but very interesting: Its weight fell exactly between the weights of calcium and barium. Even more interesting, when he looked into the chemistry of strontium, it behaved like barium and calcium in chemical reactions. Strontium was somehow a blend of two elements, one lighter and one heavier.

Excited, Döbereiner began to weigh more elements precisely, looking around for other sets of three that he called "triads." Up popped chlorine, bromine, and iodine; sulfur, selenium (element 34), and tellurium; and others. In each case, the weight of the middle element fell halfway between its chemical cousins. Convinced this was not a coincidence, Döbereiner began to group these elements into what today we'd recognize as columns of the periodic table. Indeed, the chemists who constructed the first periodic tables fifty years later started with Döbereiner's pillars.

Now, the reason fifty years passed between Döbereiner and Dmitri Mendeleev without a periodic table was that the triad work got out of hand. Instead of using strontium and its neighbors to search for a universal way to organize matter, chemists began seeing weird collections of three everywhere, and they lost focus. Nevertheless, thanks to Döbereiner, strontium was the first element correctly placed in a larger universal scheme of elements. And Döbereiner never would have figured all this out without first the faith and then the support of Goethe.

So even if Goethe made a poor show of things in his own scientific work, his writing helped spread the idea that science was noble, and he nudged chemists toward the periodic table. He deserves at least an honorary position in the history of science—which, in the end, might have satisfied him.

TWAIN'S RADIUM

Goethe wasn't the only great writer to influence the periodic table. American superstar author Mark Twain was another.

Like Goethe, Twain was fascinated by scientific discovery. He wrote short stories about inventions, technology, space and time travel, and even, in his story "Sold to Satan," the perils of the periodic table.

The story, two thousand words long, starts shortly after an economic crisis around 1904. The main character is sick of having no money, so he decides to sell his soul to the Devil. What does that have to do with the periodic table? Well, in the story, Satan is made entirely of radium!

Six years before Twain's story, Marie Curie had astounded the scientific world with her tales of radioactive elements. It was genuine news, but Twain must have been pretty plugged in to the scientific scene to incorporate all the cheeky details he did into "Sold to Satan." Radium's radioactivity charges the air around it electrically, so Satan glows a luminescent green. Also, like a warm-blooded rock, radium is always hotter than its surroundings because its radioactivity heats it up. To avoid burning the people he comes across, radium-bodied Satan wears a protective coat of polonium, another new element discovered by Curie.

Scientifically, this is rubbish: A "transparent" shell of polonium, "thin as a gelatine film," could never contain the heat of a critical mass of radium. But we'll forgive Twain, since the polonium serves a larger dramatic purpose. It gives Satan a reason to threaten, "If I should strip off my skin the world would vanish away in a flash of flame and a puff of smoke, and the remnants of the extinguished moon would sift down through space a mere snow-shower of gray ashes!"

But Twain could not let the Devil win. The trapped radium heat is so intense that Satan soon admits, "I burn. I suffer within." But, jokes aside, Twain was already trembling about the awesome power of nuclear energy in 1904. Had he lived forty years more, he surely would have shaken his head—dispirited, yet hardly surprised—to see people chasing after nuclear missiles instead of plentiful atomic energy.

Twain's story deals with the bottom of the periodic table and some of the newer elements, but of all the tales of artists and elements, none seems sadder or harsher than poet Robert Lowell's adventures with one of the oldest elements, lithium, at the very top of the table.

Lowell's Lithium

Robert Lowell was a typical "mad artist" whose genius stems from parts of the mind most people cannot access, much less use for their own artistic purposes. Unfortunately, Lowell couldn't control his madness outside the margins of his poems, and in real life he often seemed crazy. He once turned up sputtering on a friend's doorstep, convinced that he (Lowell) was the Virgin Mary. Another time, in Bloomington, Indiana, he convinced himself he could stop cars on the highway by spreading his arms wide like Jesus. In classes he taught, he wasted hours babbling and rewriting the poems of his students. At nineteen, he abandoned a fiancée and drove from Boston to the country house of a Tennessee poet who Lowell hoped would mentor him. He just assumed that the man would put him up. The poet graciously explained there was no room at the inn, so to speak, and joked that Lowell would have to camp on the lawn if he wanted to stay. Lowell nodded and left—for Sears. He bought a tent, returned to the house, and erected it on the grass.

People loved these stories, and during the 1950s and 1960s, Lowell was the most famous poet in the United States, winning prizes and selling thousands of books. Everyone thought that Lowell's antics were just those of a crazy artist being a crazy artist, but in reality, Lowell had a chemical imbalance in his brain, one that made him a manic-depressive. The public saw only the wild man, not his horrible moods—moods that badly affected his whole life. Luckily, the first real chemical mood stabilizer, lithium, came to the United States in 1967. A desperate Lowell—who'd just been placed in a psychiatric hospital—agreed to try the new medicine.

Lithium has no normal role in the body. It's not an essential mineral like iron or magnesium, or even a trace element like chromium (element 24). In fact, pure lithium is a scarily reactive metal (it catches fire when dropped in water). Nor does lithium (which in its drug form is a salt, lithium carbonate) work the way we expect drugs to. Lithium won't "cure" a bad mood, it only prevents the next mood from starting.

Lithium tweaks many mood-altering chemicals in the brain, and its effects are complicated. Most interesting, lithium seems to reset the body's rhythm, its inner clock. In chemically balanced people, the conditions around them, especially the sun, determine their mood and when they are worn out for the day. They're on a twenty-four-hour cycle. Manic-depressive, or bipolar, people run on cycles independent of the sun. And run and run. When they're feeling good, their brains flood them with happiness, and a lack of sunshine does not turn the happiness tap off. Such people barely need sleep, and their self-confidence swells. Eventually, those surges wear out the brain, and people crash. Severe manic-depressives sometimes stay in bed for weeks at a time.

Lithium helps to regulate the proteins that control the body's inner clock. It acts as "anti-sunlight" and resets the body's clock to a normal, twenty-four-hour cycle—preventing both the highs and the lows.

Lowell responded immediately to lithium. His personal life grew steadier, and at one point he pronounced himself cured. From his new, stable perspective, he could see how his old life had been so damaging. For all the moving lines within his poems, nothing Lowell ever wrote was as touching as a simple note to his publisher, Robert Giroux, after doctors started him on lithium.

"It's terrible, Bob," he said, "to think that all I've suffered, and all the suffering I've caused, might have arisen from the lack of a little salt in my brain."

Lowell felt that his life improved on lithium, but the effect of lithium on his writing was debatable. Many artists report feeling tranquilized on lithium. And his poetry undoubtedly changed after

1967. Instead of inventing lines from his wild mind, he began steal-ing lines from private letters, which outraged the people whom he quoted.

Such work won Lowell a Pulitzer Prize for writing in 1974, but compared with his younger work, it's barely read today and not thought of as his best poetry. For all that the periodic table inspired Goethe, Twain, and others, Lowell's lithium may have sustained his health but damaged his art, and made a mad genius merely human.

CHAPTER 15

AN ELEMENT OF MADNESS

ROBERT LOWELL MAY HAVE BEEN KNOWN AS A MAD ARTIST, BUT WHAT ABOUT mad scientists? The mad scientists of the periodic table were usually caught up in a special kind of madness known as pathological science. Pathological science is a strange kind of madness whereby normally reasonable and logical scientists choose some highly unlikely phenomenon that, for whatever reason, appeals to them, and then use all their scientific knowledge and skill to try to prove it true. What's really fascinating about that madness is how it can exist side by side in the same mind with brilliance.

SPIRITUALISM AND SELENIUM

Unlike almost every other scientist in this book, William Crookes, born in London in 1832, never worked at a university. The oldest of sixteen children, he later fathered ten of his own, and he supported his enormous family by writing a popular book on diamonds and editing a scientific journal called *Chemical News*. Nevertheless, Crookes did enough world-class science on elements such as selenium and thallium to get elected to England's premier scientific club, the Royal Society, in 1863, at just thirty-one years of age.

A decade later, he was almost kicked out.

His downfall began in 1867, when his brother Philip died at sea. William and the other Crookeses nearly went mad with grief. For comfort, William turned to the newly popular movement called spiritualism. Part of the spiritualist movement was the idea that you could communicate with the dead during gatherings called séances, and William was keen to get in touch with his recently deceased brother.

This wacky behavior put Crookes in the minority among his fellow scientists in the Royal Society. Knowing this, Crookes kept his beliefs secret, and in 1870, when he announced that he had drawn up a scientific study of spiritualism, most fellows of the Royal Society were delighted—they assumed he would demolish the whole idea of spiritualism in his journal.

Things did not turn out so neatly. In 1874, Crookes published a paper titled "Notes of an Enquiry into the Phenomena Called Spiritual" in a journal he owned called the *Quarterly Journal of Science*. Instead of attacking all the spiritualist mischief—"levitation," "phantoms," "percussive sounds," "luminous appearances," "the rising of tables and chairs off the ground"—he concluded that there were some "real" supernatural forces.

Coming from Crookes, this support amazed everyone in England, including the spiritualists. Crookes's fellows in the Royal Society were equally surprised but rather more upset. They argued that Crookes had been blinded by tricks and conned by charismatic mediums. They also tore into the dodgy science that he'd given in his report. A few scientists cannot forgive him to this day, and they even point to his work on the elements as proof that he went crazy. Why is that?

Well, Crookes had previously studied selenium. Though selenium is an essential trace nutrient in all animals, it is toxic in large doses. Cattle ranchers know this well. If not watched carefully, their cattle may find a prairie plant of the pea family known as locoweed, some varieties of which soak up selenium from the soil. Cattle that munch on locoweed begin to stagger and stumble and develop fevers, sores, and anorexia—a set of symptoms known as the blind staggers. The surest sign that selenium actually makes cattle go mad is that they grow addicted to locoweed despite its awful side effects, and they stop eating anything else. Overall, it's fitting that "selenium" comes from *selene*, Greek for "moon," which has links—through *luna*, Latin for "moon"—to "lunatic" and "lunacy."

Given that, it may make sense to blame Crookes's delusions

on selenium, but some inconvenient facts get in the way. Selenium often attacks within a week; Crookes got goofy in early middle age, long after he'd stopped working with selenium. Plus, many biochemists now think that other chemicals in locoweed contribute just as much to the craziness and intoxication of the cattle. Finally, in a clinching clue that selenium did not influence Crookes, his beard never fell out, a classic symptom of selenium poisoning.

A full beard also suggests that Crookes was not driven mad by another poisonous element on the periodic table—the poisoner's poison, thallium. Crookes discovered thallium at age twenty-six (a finding that all but ensured his election to the Royal Society) and continued to play with it in his lab for a decade. But he apparently never inhaled enough even to lose his whiskers. Crookes actually gave up his spiritualist ideas after 1874, rededicating himself to science, and major discoveries lay ahead. He was the first to suggest the existence of isotopes (atoms of the same element with a different number of neutrons). He built vital new scientific equipment and confirmed the presence of helium in rocks, its first detection on Earth. In 1897, the newly knighted Sir William dived into radioactivity, even discovering (though without realizing it) element 91, protactinium, in 1900.

As such, the best explanation for Crookes's getting mixed up in spiritualism was that, ruined by grief for his brother, he was taken in by pathological science, not that selenium or thallium drove him mad.

Shark Teeth

A pathological science takes advantage of the researcher's caution. Basically, its believers use the ambiguity about evidence *as* evidence—claiming that, because scientists do not know everything, there is room for their pet theory, too. That's exactly what happened with manganese (element 25) and the megalodon.

This story starts in 1873, when the research vessel HMS *Challenger* set out from England to explore the Pacific Ocean. In a wonderfully low-tech setup, the crew dropped overboard huge buckets tied to ropes three miles long and dredged the ocean floor. In addition to fantastical fish and other critters, they hauled up dozens upon dozens of spherical rocks shaped like fossilized potatoes and solid, mineralized ice-cream cones. These hunks, mostly manganese, appeared all over the seabed in every part of the ocean, meaning there had to be untold billions of them scattered around the world.

That was the first surprise. The second happened when the crew cracked open the cones: the manganese had formed around giant shark teeth. The biggest, most freakish shark teeth today run about two and a half inches max. The manganese-covered teeth stretched five or more inches—mouth talons capable of shattering bone like an ax. Using the same basic techniques as with dinosaur fossils, paleontologists determined (just from the teeth!) that this ancient Jaws, dubbed the megalodon, grew to approximately fifty feet, weighed approximately fifty tons, and could swim approximately fifty miles per hour. It could probably close its mouth of 250 teeth with a megaton force, and it fed mostly on primitive whales in shallow, tropical waters. It probably died out when its prey migrated permanently to colder, deeper waters, an environment that didn't suit its high metabolism and ravenous appetite.

All fine science so far. The pathology started with the manganese. Shark teeth litter the ocean floor because they're about the hardest biological substance known, the only part of shark carcasses that survive the crush of the deep ocean (most sharks have cartilage for skeletons). It's not clear why manganese, of all the dissolved metals in the ocean, covers shark teeth, but scientists know roughly how quickly it accumulates: between one-half and one and a half millimeters per millennium. From that rate they have determined that the vast majority of recovered teeth date back at least 1.5 million years, meaning the megalodons probably died out around then.

But—and here was the breach into which some people rushed— some megalodon teeth had mysteriously thin manganese plaque, about eleven thousand years' worth. Evolutionarily, that's an awfully short time. And, really, what's to say scientists won't soon find one from ten thousand years ago? Or eight thousand years ago? Or later?

You can see where this thinking leads. In the 1960s, a few enthusiasts with *Jurassic Park* imaginations grew convinced that rogue megalodons still lurk in the oceans. "Megalodon lives!" they cried. And like rumors about UFOs and Area 51, the legend has never quite died. The most common tale is that megalodons have evolved to become deep-sea divers and now spend their days fighting krakens in the black depths. Like Crookes's phantoms, megalodons are *supposed* to be elusive, an explanation that gives people a convenient escape when pressed on why the giant sharks are so scarce nowadays.

There's probably not a person alive who, deep down, doesn't hope that megalodons still haunt the seas. Unfortunately, the idea crumbles under scrutiny. Among other things, the teeth with thin layers of manganese were almost certainly torn up from old bedrock beneath the ocean floor (where they accumulated no manganese) and exposed to water only recently. They're probably much older than eleven thousand years. And although there have been eyewitness accounts of the beasts, they're all from sailors, notorious storytellers, and the megalodons in their stories vary manically in size and shape. One all-white Moby Dick shark stretched up to three hundred feet long! (Funny, though, no one thought to snap a picture.) Overall, such stories, as with Crookes's testimony about supernatural beings, depend on subjective interpretations, and without objective evidence, it's not plausible to conclude that megalodons, even a few of them, slipped through evolution's snares.

But what really makes the ongoing hunt for megalodons pathological is that doubt from the establishment only deepens people's convictions. Instead of refuting the manganese findings, they counterattack with heroic tales of rebels, rogues who proved squaresville scientists wrong in the past. They invariably bring up the coelacanth, a primitive deep-sea fish once thought to have gone extinct eighty million years ago, until it turned up in a fish market in South Africa in 1938. According to this logic, because scientists were wrong about the coelacanth, they might be wrong about the megalodon, too. And "might" is all the megalodon lovers need. For their theories about its survival aren't based on a preponderance of evidence, but on an emotional attachment: the hope, the need, for something fantastic to be true.

RÖNTGEN'S RAYS

Not every scientist with a touch of madness ends up drowning in pathological science, of course. Some, like Crookes, escape and go on to do great work. And then there are the rare cases where what seems like pathological science at the beginning actually turns out to be REAL science in the end!

Wilhelm Röntgen tried very hard to prove himself wrong while experimenting with invisible rays, but he couldn't.

In November 1895, Röntgen was playing around in his laboratory in central Germany with a Crookes tube, an important new tool for studying subatomic phenomena. Named after its inventor, you know who, the Crookes tube was a vacuum in a glass bulb with two metal plates inside at either end. Running a current between the plates caused a beam to leap across the vacuum, a crackle of light like something from a special-effects lab. Scientists now know it's a beam of electrons, but in 1895, Röntgen and others were trying to figure that out.

A colleague of Röntgen had found that when he made a Crookes tube with a small aluminium foil window in the glass, the beam would tunnel through the foil out into the air. It died pretty quickly—air was like poison to the beam—but it could light up a green phosphorescent screen a few inches away. Röntgen repeated the experiment in 1895, but with some alterations. Instead of leaving his Crookes tube naked, he covered it with black paper, so that the beam would escape *only* through the foil window. And instead of the phosphorescing chemicals his colleague had used, he painted his plates with a barium compound.

Accounts of what happened next vary, but basically every time he turned the current on, a barium plate would glow. But the crazy thing was that the plate was not located near the Crookes tube—it was clear across the laboratory!

Röntgen confirmed that no light was escaping from the blackened Crookes tube. He'd been sitting in a dark lab, so that sunshine couldn't have caused the glow, either. But he also knew the Crookes beams couldn't survive long enough in air to jump over to the barium plates sitting far away from the tube. He later admitted he thought he was imagining things—the tube was obviously the cause, but he knew of nothing that could travel through the black paper. It was a mystery.

So Röntgen continued to experiment. He propped up a barium-coated screen and put the nearest objects at hand, like a book, near the tube to block the beam. To his amazement, an outline of a key he used as a bookmark appeared on the screen. He could somehow *see through things*. The truly black-magic moment came when he held up another object—and saw the bones of his own hand! At this point, Röntgen thought he'd gone stark raving mad! Far from it—he had actually discovered X-rays.

Interestingly, instead of leaping to the convenient conclusion that he'd discovered something completely new, Röntgen assumed he'd made a mistake somewhere. Embarrassed, and determined to prove himself wrong, he locked himself in his lab for seven weeks. He dismissed his assistants and took his meals grudgingly, gulping down food and grunting more than talking to his family. Unlike

Crookes, Röntgen tried to fit his findings in with known physics. He didn't want to be revolutionary or claim that he had discovered something new. He even tried hard to disprove himself. But the Crookes tube lit up the barium plates every time, despite his doubts.

At last, slightly more confident that he was seeing something real, he brought his wife into the lab one afternoon and exposed her hand to the X-rays. When she saw her bones, she freaked out, thinking it was a premonition of her death. She refused to go back into his haunted lab after that, but her reaction brought huge relief to Röntgen—it proved that he hadn't imagined it all.

At that point, Röntgen announced his "röntgen rays." Naturally, people doubted him, just as they'd doubted Crookes. But Röntgen had been patient and modest, and every time someone objected, he countered by saying he'd already investigated that possibility, until his colleagues had no more objections. And here is the uplifting side to the normally severe tales of pathological science.

Scientists can be cruel to new ideas. One can imagine them asking, "What sort of 'mystery beams' can fly invisibly through black paper, Wilhelm, and light up the bones in your body? *Nonsense.*" But when he fought back with solid proof, with repeatable experiments, most threw out their old ideas and embraced his. Though an ordinary professor his whole life, Röntgen became every scientist's hero. In 1901, he won the first Nobel Prize in Physics. Two decades later, physicist Henry Moseley used his electron gun and some X-ray detectors to revolutionize the study of the periodic table. Even better, in 2004, element 111 was named roentgenium in Wilhelm's honor.

PART V

ELEMENT SCIENCE
TODAY AND
TOMORROW

CHAPTER 16

CHEMISTRY WAY, WAY BELOW ZERO

RÖNTGEN REMINDED SCIENTISTS THAT THE PERIODIC TABLE IS FULL OF SURPRISES. There's always something new to discover about the elements, even today. But with most of the easy discoveries already made by Röntgen's time, making new discoveries required drastic measures. Scientists had to place the elements under severe conditions—especially extreme cold, which can cause some strange behavior. Extreme cold doesn't always work out too well for the humans making the discoveries, either.

NOT COOL, TIN

By 1911, no human being had ever reached the South Pole. This led to an epic race among explorers to get there first—and leads us to a cautionary tale about what can go wrong with chemistry at extreme temperatures.

That year was chilly, even by Antarctic standards, but a band of Englishmen led by Robert Falcon Scott nonetheless determined that they would be the first to reach the pole.

After slogging across the ice for months on foot, five men, led by Scott, arrived at the South Pole in January 1912—only to find a tent, a Norwegian flag, and an annoyingly friendly letter. Scott had lost out to the Norwegian explorer Roald Amundsen, whose team had arrived a whole month earlier. In his diary, Scott wrote: "Great God! This is an awful place. Now for the run home and a desperate struggle. I wonder if we can do it."

The return trip for Scott and his team would have been difficult anyway, but Antarctica threw everything at them it could to punish and harass them. They were marooned for weeks in a monsoon of snow flurries, and their journals, discovered later, showed that they faced starvation, scurvy, dehydration, hypothermia, and gangrene. But worse was the lack of heating fuel.

Scott had traveled through the Arctic the year before and had found that the leather seals on his canisters of kerosene fuel had leaked badly. He'd routinely lost half his fuel. For the South Pole run, his team had experimented with sealing cans with melted tin. But on the return trip, when his men reached the canisters awaiting them, they found many of them were empty. In a double blow, the fuel had often leaked into their food supply and destroyed it.

Without kerosene for fuel, the men couldn't cook food or melt ice to drink. One of them became ill and died; another went insane in the extreme cold and simply wandered off. The last three, including Scott, pushed on. They officially died of exposure in late March 1912, eleven miles short of the British base.

In his day, Scott was wildly popular, especially in Britain. The British received the news of his death very badly, and as a result, people have always tried to excuse him from blame; the periodic table provided a convenient excuse.

Tin, which Scott used to seal the cans of fuel, has been a prized metal since biblical times because it is so easy to shape. Ironically, the better people got at refining and purifying tin, the worse it became for everyday use. Whenever pure tin tools or tin coins or tin toys got cold, a whitish "rust" appeared on the surface of the metal. The white "rust" would then weaken and corrode the tin, until it crumbled and eroded.

Unlike iron rust, this was not a chemical reaction. As scientists now know, this happens because tin atoms can arrange themselves inside a solid in two different ways, and when they get cold, they shift from their strong "beta" form to the white, crumbly, powdery "alpha" form.

To visualize the difference, imagine stacking atoms in a huge crate like oranges. The bottom of the crate is lined with a single layer of oranges. To fill the second, third, and fourth layers, you might balance each orange right on top of one in the first layer. That's one form, or crystal structure. Or you might put the second layer of oranges into the spaces between the oranges in the first layer, then the third layer into the spaces between the oranges in the second layer, and so on. That creates a second crystal structure with a different density and different properties. These are just two of the many ways to pack oranges together. As it turns out, it works exactly the same way with atoms.

What Scott's men found out the hard way is that an element's atoms can shift from a weak crystal structure to a strong one, or vice versa. Usually it takes extreme conditions for the rearrangement to happen, just as extreme heat and pressure can turn carbon from black graphite into shiny diamonds. Unfortunately, tin can change at a temperature of just 56°F. Even the temperature of a cool evening in October can start the process, and lower temperatures can make it happen much, much faster. Any slight damage to the surface of the metal (such as dents from canisters being tossed onto hard-packed ice) can speed up the change. It gets even worse.

The condition is sometimes called tin leprosy because it burrows deep inside the metal like a disease. The beta–alpha shift can even release enough energy to cause sound—yes, you can actually hear

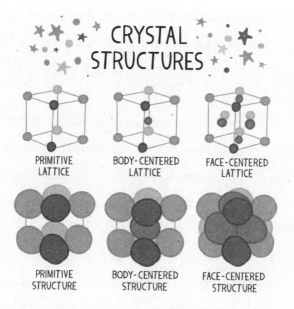

CRYSTAL STRUCTURES

PRIMITIVE LATTICE

BODY-CENTERED LATTICE

FACE-CENTERED LATTICE

PRIMITIVE STRUCTURE

BODY-CENTERED STRUCTURE

FACE-CENTERED STRUCTURE

the metal groaning. This is sometimes called "tin scream" although in reality it sounds more like radio static.

The beta–alpha change of tin has been a convenient chemical scapegoat throughout history. Various European cities with harsh winters (such as Saint Petersburg, Russia) have legends about expensive tin pipes on new church organs exploding into ash as soon as the organist hit the keys.

Then there was Napoleon. When he stupidly attacked Russia in June 1812 and had to retreat during a brutal cold snap a few months later, the tin buttons on his men's jackets reportedly cracked apart (though many historians dispute this) and left the Frenchmen's inner garments exposed every time the wind kicked up. As with the horrible circumstances faced by Scott and his men, the French army was going to have a difficult time in Russia anyway. But element 50's shifting structure perhaps made things tougher, and chemistry proved an easier thing to blame than Napoleon's bad judgment.

There's no doubt that Scott's men found empty canisters—that fact is written in his diary—but it is not known for sure whether the disintegration of the tin caused the leaks. Tin leprosy makes sense, but canisters from other teams discovered decades later retained their seals. Scott did use purer tin—although it would have to have been extremely pure for leprosy to take hold. Yet no other good explanation besides sabotage exists, and there's no evidence of foul play. Either way, Scott and his men died on the ice, victims at least in part of the periodic table.

Organizing Atoms

Odd things can happen when matter gets very cold and shifts from one state to another. You may know about three common states of matter: solid, liquid, and gas. There are other states of matter that don't get as much attention in school—things like plasma, superfluids, and degenerate matter, all of which have unique properties. (You may also wonder why Jell-O doesn't count as its own special state. The answer? Colloids like Jell-O are blends of two states. The water and gelatin mixture may be thought of as either a highly flexible solid or a superthick liquid.)

The point is that the universe can contain far more states of matter—different arrangements of particles—than are dreamed of in our simple categories of solid, liquid, and gas. Albert Einstein uncovered a new state of matter while fiddling around with a few quantum mechanics equations in 1924—then dismissed his calculations and his theoretical discovery as too weird to ever exist. Until someone actually made it in 1995!

In some ways, solids are the most basic state of matter. In solids, atoms line up in a repetitive, three-dimensional structure, though even the most ordinary solids can usually form more than one type of crystal. Scientists can now shape ice into fifteen different types of crystals by using high-pressure chambers. Some ices sink rather than float in water, and others form not six-sided snowflakes but shapes like palm leaves or heads of cauliflower. One alien ice, Ice X, doesn't melt until it reaches 3,700°F. Even chemicals as impure and complicated as chocolate form weird structures that can shift shapes the way tin does. Ever opened an old Hershey's Kiss and found a white colored haze on the surface of the chocolate? It's just sugar or cocoa butter, but we might call that chocolate leprosy, caused by the same beta–alpha shifts that Scott found in tin in Antarctica.

CHAPTER 17

THE SCIENCE OF BUBBLES

BUBBLES HAVE PROVED USEFUL IN MANY AREAS OF SCIENCE, BUT ONLY AROUND 1900 did bubble science become a respectable field. The men responsible, however, Ernest Rutherford and Lord Kelvin (William Thomson), had only vague ideas of what their work would lead to.

BUBBLY INSPIRATION

Rutherford moved from New Zealand to the University of Cambridge in 1895, and he devoted himself to radioactivity. Nobody was better, possibly in the history of science, at extracting nature's secrets out of experiments. And there's no better example than the elegance he used to solve the mystery of how one element can transform into another.

After moving from Cambridge to Montreal, Rutherford grew interested in how radioactive substances fill the air around them with even more radioactivity. To investigate this, Rutherford built on the work of Marie Curie. According to Curie (among others), radioactive elements leaked a sort of gas of "pure radioactivity" that charged the air, just as lightbulbs flood the air with light. Rutherford suspected that "pure radioactivity" was actually an unknown gaseous element with its own radioactive properties.

To investigate his theory, Rutherford let nature do the work for him. He simply let a sample of radioactive metal decay in a closed container, then drew bubbles of the gas into an inverted flask, a procedure that gave him all the radioactive material he needed. Rutherford and his lab partner, Frederick Soddy, quickly proved the radioactive bubbles were in fact a new element, radon. And because the sample beneath the inverted beaker got smaller in exactly the same proportion as the radon sample grew in volume, they realized that one element actually changed into the other.

Not only did Rutherford and Soddy find a new element, they discovered that as elements decayed, they could jump around the periodic table, and that they could skip across boxes on the table. This change from one element into another is called transmutation. It was thrilling, but it also presented a problem. Science had spent a huge amount of time and effort discrediting those old chemical magicians, the alchemists, who'd claimed that they could turn lead into gold—and here were Rutherford and Soddy, saying that, yes, something like that seemed possible!

Rutherford had named the little bits that flew off radioactive atoms alpha particles. (He also discovered beta particles.) He suspected that alpha particles were actually helium atoms breaking off and escaping like bubbles through a boiling liquid. To test this idea, Rutherford obtained two glass bulbs. One was soap-bubble thin, and he pumped radon into it. The other was thicker and larger, and it surrounded the first. The alpha particles had enough energy to tunnel through the first, thin glass shell but not the thicker second, so they became trapped in the vacuum cavity between the two bulbs.

After a few days, this wasn't much of an experiment, since the trapped alpha particles were colorless and didn't really do anything. But then Rutherford ran a battery current through the cavity. If you've ever traveled to Tokyo or New York and looked around at the signs, you know what happened. Helium, like all noble gases, glows when excited by electricity, and Rutherford's mystery particles began glowing helium's characteristic green and yellow. Rutherford basically proved that alpha particles were escaped helium atoms with an early "neon" light.

Rutherford announced the alpha-helium connection during his acceptance speech for the 1908 Nobel Prize. (In addition to winning the prize himself, Rutherford mentored and trained eleven future prizewinners, the last in 1978, more than four decades after he died.) Rutherford later ended up as scientific royalty, too, with his own box on the periodic table, element 104, rutherfordium.

LORD KELVIN'S LASTING IMPACT

Lord Kelvin popularized bubble science by saying things like he could spend a lifetime scrutinizing a single soap bubble. That was actually a lie, since, according to his lab notebooks, Kelvin came up with the outline of his bubble work one lazy morning in bed, and he produced just one short paper on it. Still, there are wonderful stories of this white-bearded Victorian splashing around in basins of water and glycerin, making strings of interlocking, square bubbles.

Kelvin's work would inspire bubble science in future generations, too. Biologist D'Arcy Wentworth Thompson applied Kelvin's ideas about bubble formation to cell development in his hugely important 1917 book *On Growth and Form*. The modern field of cell biology began at this point. What's more, recent biochemical research hints that bubbles were the cause of life itself. The first complex organic molecules may have formed not in the ocean, as is commonly thought, but in water bubbles trapped in Arctic-like sheets of ice. Water is quite heavy, and when it freezes, it crushes together dissolved "impurities," such as organic molecules, inside bubbles. The concentration and compression in those bubbles might have been high enough to fuse those molecules into living cells.

Kelvin's work also inspired military science. During World War I, another lord, Lord Rayleigh, took on the urgent wartime problem of why submarine propellers were disintegrating, even when the rest of the hull remained intact. It turned out that bubbles produced by the churning propellers turned around and attacked the metal blades the way sugar attacks teeth.

These days, physicists interested in alternative energy model superconductors with bubbles. Pathologists describe AIDS as a "foamy" virus, for the way infected cells swell before exploding. Entomologists (scientists who study insects) know of bugs that use bubbles like submersibles to breathe underwater, and ornithologists (scientists who study birds) know that the metallic shine of peacocks' plumage comes from light tickling bubbles in the feathers. Most important, in 2008, in food science, students at Appalachian State University finally determined what makes Diet Coke explode when you drop Mentos into it. Bubbles. The grainy surface of Mentos candy acts as a net to grab small dissolved bubbles, which combine to form larger ones. Eventually, a few gigantic bubbles break off, rocket upward, and whoosh through the nozzle of the bottle, spurting up to twenty magnificent feet. Clearly, this discovery was one of the greatest moments in bubble science....

CHAPTER 18

TOOLS OF RIDICULOUS PRECISION

SOME SCIENTISTS AND SCIENCE TEACHERS CAN BE VERY EXACT. THEY MAY TAKE points off a test score if the sixth decimal place in your answer was rounded incorrectly; they may tuck in their periodic table T-shirt, and insist on correcting those who say "weight" when they meant "mass"; and they may make everyone, including themselves, wear goggles even while mixing sugar water. Now try to imagine someone whom this scientist would hate for being even MORE fussy. *That* is the kind of person who works for a bureau of standards and measurement.

MAINTAINING MEASUREMENTS

Most countries have a standards bureau, whose job it is to measure *everything*. To scientists who work at standards bureaus, measurement isn't just a practice that makes science possible; it's a science in itself.

For historical reasons, France's Bureau International des Poids et Mesures (BIPM), just outside Paris, acts as the boss of all the other standards bureaus, making sure all the "franchises" stay in line. One of the more wacky jobs of the BIPM is looking after the International Prototype of the Kilogram—the world's official kilogram. It's a two-inch-wide, 90 percent platinum cylinder that, by definition, has a mass of exactly 1.000000...kilogram (to as many decimal places as you like). I'd say that's about two pounds, but I'd feel guilty about not being *exactly* right.

Because the International Prototype of the Kilogram is a physical object and therefore may be damaged, and because the definition of a kilogram has to stay constant, the BIPM must make sure it never gets scratched, never attracts a speck of dust, and never loses (the bureau hopes!) a single atom. So they constantly monitor the Kilogram's temperature and the pressure to prevent microscopic changes and any stress that could knock off even a single atom. And the Kilogram is made from dense platinum (and iridium, element 77) to minimize the surface area exposed to dirty air. Platinum also conducts electricity well, a property that cuts down on the buildup of static electricity that may zap some stray atoms.

Finally, platinum's toughness helps prevent the chance of a disastrous fingernail scratch on those rare occasions when people actually need to lay a hand on the Kilogram. Other countries need their own official 1.000000...cylinder to avoid having to fly to Paris every time they want to measure something precisely, and since the Kilogram is *the* standard, each country's copy has to be compared against it. (The process of comparison to make sure everything is exactly correct is called calibration.) The United States has its own official kilogram, called K20 (i.e., the twentieth official copy), which is kept in a government building in Maryland.

Usually, the BIPM uses one of six official copies of the Kilogram (each kept under two bell jars) to calibrate the copies. But the official copies have to be measured against their own standard—the original—so every few years scientists remove the Kilogram from its vault (using tongs and wearing latex gloves, of course, and not holding it for too long, because the person's body temperature could heat it up and ruin everything) and calibrate the calibrators. Alarmingly, scientists noticed during calibrations in the 1990s that, even accounting for atoms that rub off when people touch it, in the past few decades the Kilogram had lost an additional mass equal to that of a fingerprint (!), half a microgram per year. No one knows why.

The failure to keep the Kilogram perfect is worrying, and it would be best if we could get rid of the cylinder altogether. Science owes much of its progress since about 1600 to using a non-human-centered point of view about the universe. The kilogram is one of seven "base units" of measurement used in science (the others being the ampere, the candela, the meter, the kelvin, the mole, and the second), and it's no longer acceptable for any of those units to be based on a human-created object such as the platinum-and-iridium cylinder—especially if it's mysteriously shrinking. The kilogram conundrum has become an increasing source of international worry and embarrassment (at least for the people who make it their business to worry about such things!).

WHAT DO THE MEASUREMENTS MEASURE . . . ?

There are seven so-called fundamental units that scientists use to measure things in the world around us:

Ampere: Electric current
Candela: Luminous intensity
Meter: Length
Kelvin: Temperature
Mole: The number of atoms in a given amount of a substance
Second: Time
Kilogram: Mass

The pain is even worse because the kilogram is the last base unit that is connected to a physical object. A platinum rod in Paris defined 1.000000...meter through much of the twentieth century, until scientists redefined it with a krypton atom in 1960, fixing the meter as being 1,650,763.73 wavelengths of red-orange light from a krypton-86 atom. This distance is virtually identical to the length of the old rod, but it meant that the old rod could be scrapped, since that many wavelengths of krypton light would stretch the same distance in any vacuum anywhere without having to worry about handling a physical object. Since then, measurement scientists (metrologists) have re-redefined a meter as the distance any light travels in a vacuum in 1/299,792,458 of a second.

In the same way, the official definition of one second used to be about 1/86,400 of one spin on Earth's axis (86,400 being the number of seconds in one day). But a few pesky facts made that an inconvenient standard. Most important, the length of a day is slowly increasing because of the sloshing of ocean tides, which drag and slow Earth's rotation. To correct for this, metrologists slip in a "leap second" about every third year, usually when no one's paying attention, at midnight on December 31. But that's an ugly solution, so the US standards bureau has developed cesium-based atomic clocks to define the second instead.

Atomic clocks run on the same leaping and crashing of excited electrons we've discussed before. Each cycle of jumping up and down always takes the exact same (extremely short) amount of time, so the atomic clock can measure time simply by counting the light rays that are released as the electrons move about.

Element 55 proved to be a convenient one for use in atomic clocks because it has one electron exposed in its outermost shell, with no nearby electrons to mess up the process. Cesium's outer electron is fast. Instead of a few dozen or few thousand times per second, it performs 9,192,631,770 back-and-forths every one-Mississippi, and the time that it takes for those 9,192,631,770 flip-flops is now fixed as the official standard for one second.

A Changing Constant

Scientists love constants. The charge of the electron, the strength of gravity, the speed of light—no matter the experiment, no matter the circumstances, those values never vary. If they did, scientists would have to throw out the precision that separates "hard" sciences from social sciences such as economics, where human behaviors (and human idiocy) make universal, unbreakable laws impossible.

Even more interesting to scientists are what are known as fundamental constants. Obviously, the numerical value of your height or weight or anything else would change if we suddenly decided that meters should be longer or if the kilogram suddenly shrank. Fundamental constants, however, don't depend on measurement.

The best known of these fundamental constants is called the fine-structure constant, which is related to electrons. In short, it controls all kinds of processes within atoms. In fact, if alpha (that's what scientists call the fine-structure constant) had been slightly smaller right after the big bang, nuclear fusion in stars would never have gotten hot enough to create carbon. Also, if alpha had grown slightly larger, all carbon atoms would have disintegrated long before finding their way into us. Why it didn't get too big or too small is, as physicist Richard Feynman once said, "...one of the greatest damn mysteries of physics: a magic number that comes to us with no understanding by man. You might say the 'hand of God' wrote that number, and we don't know how He pushed His pencil."

Historically, that didn't stop people from trying to work out a value for the fine-structure constant. English astronomer Arthur Eddington grew fascinated with alpha. Eddington believed that some numbers had supernatural significance, and in the early 1900s, after alpha was measured to be around 1/136, Eddington began making up "proofs" that alpha equaled exactly 1/136, partly because he found a mathematical link between 136 and 666 (a.k.a., the "sign of the beast," a number associated with the devil). Later measurements showed that alpha was closer to 1/137, but Eddington just tossed a 1 into his formula somewhere and continued on. This earned him the nickname "Sir Arthur Adding-One."

Today alpha equals 1/137.0359 or so, and its value makes the periodic table possible. It allows atoms to exist and also allows them to react with sufficient energy to form compounds, since electrons neither roam too far from their nuclei nor cling too closely. This just-right balance has led many scientists to conclude that the universe couldn't have hit upon its fine-structure constant by accident. Those who prefer theology (the study of religion) over science say alpha proves that a creator has "programmed" the universe to produce both molecules and, possibly, life. That's why it was such a big deal in 1976 when a Soviet (now American) scientist named Alexander Shlyakhter visited a place in the African nation of Gabon called Oklo and declared that alpha was getting bigger.

Oklo is the only *natural* nuclear fission reactor known to exist. It stirred to life some 1.7 billion years ago, and when the French found the site in 1972, it caused a scientific roar. Oklo was powered by nothing but uranium, water, and blue-green algae (i.e., pond scum). Really. Algae in a river near Oklo produced excess oxygen after undergoing photosynthesis. The oxygen made the water so acidic that, as it trickled underground through loose soil, it dissolved the uranium from the rocks below. The uranium became concentrated in one spot, achieving a critical mass, and the water helped to slow down neutrons enough to make the nuclear fission occur.

Of course, fission also produces heat, and the reason there's not a big hole in Africa at Oklo today is that when the uranium got hot, it boiled the water away. With no water, the process ground to a halt. Only when the uranium cooled down did water trickle back in, which restarted the reactor. And the cycle repeated.

How did scientists work all this out 1.7 billion years after it happened? With elements, of course! Elements are mixed thoroughly in the Earth's crust, so the ratios of different isotopes should be the same everywhere. At Oklo, the uranium-235 concentration was 0.003 to 0.3 percent less than normal—a huge difference. In addition to that odd observation, there was an overabundance of useless elements, such as neodymium (element 60). Neodymium mostly comes in three even-numbered flavors, isotopes with masses of 142, 144, and 146. Uranium fission reactors produce odd-numbered neodymium at higher rates than normal. In fact, when scientists analyzed the neodymium at Oklo and subtracted out the natural neodymium, they found that Oklo's nuclear "signature" matched that of a modern, man-made fission reactor. Amazing.

Still, if neodymium matched, other elements didn't. When Shlyakhter compared the Oklo nuclear waste with modern waste in 1976, he found that too little of some types of samarium had formed. By itself, that's not so thrilling. But again, elements such as samarium don't just fail to form. So the missing samarium suggested to Shlyakhter that something had been off back then. He calculated that if the fine-structure constant had been just a fraction smaller when Oklo went nuclear, the differences would have been easy to explain. The problem was, alpha is a fundamental constant. It *can't* vary, not according to physics.

With so much at stake, many scientists since 1976 have challenged the alpha-Oklo link. The changes they're measuring are tiny, and after 1.7 billion years, it seems unlikely anyone will ever prove anything about alpha using Oklo data. But again, never underestimate the value of throwing an idea out there. Shlyakhter's samarium work whetted the appetite of dozens of ambitious physicists who wanted to knock off old theories, and the study of changing constants is now an active field.

Where Is Everybody?

We've already met Enrico Fermi under rather poor circumstances, since he won a Nobel Prize for discovering elements he didn't actually discover. But it isn't right just to leave you with a negative impression of him. Scientists loved Fermi universally and without reserve. He's the namesake of element 100, fermium, and he had a devilishly quick mind as well. During scientific meetings with colleagues, they sometimes needed to run to their offices to look up equations; often as not, when they returned, Fermi, unable to wait, had derived the entire equation from scratch and had the answer they needed.

Not even Fermi, however, could wrap his head around one simple question. As noted earlier, many philosophers marvel that the universe seems fine-tuned to produce life because certain fundamental constants have a "perfect" value. Moreover, scientists have long believed that Earth is not special. Given that ordinariness, as well as the infinite numbers of stars and planets, and the amount of time that has passed since the big bang, the universe should really be swarming with life. Yet not only have we never met alien creatures, we've never even gotten a hello. As Fermi thought about those contradictory facts over lunch one day, he cried out to his colleagues, as if expecting an answer, "Then where is everybody?"

His colleagues burst out laughing at what's now known as "Fermi's paradox." But other scientists took Fermi seriously, and they really believed they could get at an answer. The best-known attempt came in 1961, when astrophysicist Frank Drake laid out what is now known as the Drake equation. In short, it's a series of guesses: about how many stars exist in the galaxy, what fraction of those have Earth-like planets, what fraction of those planets have intelligent life, what fraction of those life-forms would want to make contact, and so on. Drake originally calculated that ten such civilizations exist in our galaxy. But again, that was just an informed guess. How on Earth, for instance, can we figure out what percent of aliens want to chat with us?

Nonetheless, the Drake equation is important: It outlines what data astronomers need to collect, and it put astrobiology on a scientific foundation. Perhaps someday we'll look back on it as we do early attempts to organize a periodic table. And with vast improvements recently in telescopes and other measuring devices, astrobiologists have tools to provide more than guesses. In fact, the Hubble Space Telescope and others have collected so much information from so little data that astrobiologists can now go one better than Drake. They don't have to wait for intelligent alien life to seek us out. Rather, they may be able to measure direct evidence of life by searching for elements such as magnesium.

Obviously, magnesium is less important to life than oxygen or carbon, but element 12 can be a huge help for primitive creatures, allowing organic molecules to turn into real life-forms. Almost all life-forms use metallic elements in small amounts to create, store, or move energetic molecules around inside them. Animals use iron in hemoglobin, but the earliest and most successful forms of life, especially blue-green algae, used magnesium to drive photosynthesis. Photosynthesis—the conversion of sunlight into sugars—is the basis of the food chain, and the key molecule in this process is chlorophyll, which has magnesium ions at its center.

Magnesium on planets also suggests the presence of liquid H_2O, another substance crucial for life to exist. Magnesium compounds sponge up water, so even on bare, rocky planets like Mars, there's hope of finding bacteria. On watery worlds, like Jupiter's moon Europa, magnesium helps keep oceans fluid. Europa has an icy outer crust, but there are huge liquid oceans beneath that, and satellite evidence suggests that those oceans might be full of magnesium salts. Magnesium compounds (among others) can provide the raw materials to build life. Detecting magnesium salts on a bare, airless planet is a good sign that perhaps some life-form may be there.

Even though the hunt for alien life has grown more sophisticated, it still relies on one huge assumption: that the same science we study on Earth holds true in other galaxies, and that it held true at other times. But if alpha changed over time, then perhaps life started effortlessly when alpha "relaxed" enough to allow stable carbon atoms to form, and without any need for a creator. Some physicists, using Einstein's theories, believe that alpha variations over time could mean alpha variations across space. According to this theory, just as life arose on Earth and not the moon because Earth has water and oxygen, perhaps life arose here, on a random planet in an unremarkable pocket of space, because only here does alpha have the correct value for stable atoms and full molecules. This would answer Fermi's paradox—nobody has come calling because nobody's out there.

Astronomers now know of thousands of planets, which makes the odds of finding life somewhere else quite good. Still, the great debate of astrobiology will be deciding whether Earth and human beings have a special place in the universe. Hunting for alien life will take every bit of measuring genius we have, possibly with some overlooked box on the periodic table.

CHAPTER 19

ABOVE (AND BEYOND) THE PERIODIC TABLE

THERE'S A RIDDLE AT THE FAR END OF THE PERIODIC TABLE. HIGHLY RADIOACTIVE elements are always pretty rare, so you may think that the element that falls apart the most easily would also be the rarest of all. That element, number 87, ultrafragile francium, is indeed very rare—yet one element is even rarer. To explain this, we have to explore what nuclear physicists call the "island of stability," which is their best and perhaps only hope for extending the table beyond its current size.

THE ISLAND OF STABILITY

As we know, about 90 percent of particles in the universe are hydrogen, and roughly the other 10 percent are helium. Everything else, including six million billion billion kilograms of Earth, is ultra-tiny in comparison. And in those six million billion billion kilos, the total amount of astatine (element 85), the rarest of all natural elements, is one ounce. One stupid ounce!

To give you some idea of the scale, imagine that you were looking for a particular car in a huge parking garage and you have zero idea where it is. Then imagine walking down every row, on every level, past every space, looking for your vehicle. To mimic hunting for astatine atoms inside the Earth, that parking garage would have to be about 100 million spaces wide, have 100 million rows, and be 100 million stories high.

If astatine is so rare, it's natural to ask how scientists ever found any of it at ALL. The answer is, they cheated a little. Any astatine that was originally present in the early Earth has long since decayed away through radioactivity, but other radioactive elements sometimes decay into astatine after they spit out alpha or beta particles. By knowing the total amount of the parent elements (usually elements near uranium) and by performing some calculations, scientists can get a pretty good idea about how many astatine atoms exist. This works for other elements, too. For instance, at least twenty to thirty ounces of astatine's near neighbor on the periodic table, francium, exist at any moment.

Oddly, even though astatine is much more rare than francium, it is more stable. If you had a million atoms of the longest-lived isotope of astatine, half of them would decay away in four hundred minutes. A similar sample of francium would hang on for just twenty minutes. Francium is so fragile, it's basically useless, and scientists could never gather together enough atoms of it to make a visible sample. If they did, it would be so intensely radioactive that it would murder them immediately. Most likely, no one will ever produce a visible sample of astatine, either, but at least it's good for something—as a quick-acting radioisotope in medicine.

The odd relationship between astatine and francium begins in their nuclei. There, as in all atoms, two forces compete against each other: the strong nuclear force (which is always attractive) and the electrostatic force (which can be attractive but can also repel if both of the charges involved are positive or if both are negative). Though it's the most powerful of nature's four fundamental forces, the strong nuclear force can act over only extremely short distances. If particles stray more than a few trillionths of an inch apart, the strong force loses its grip on them. When it does work (inside the nucleus, for example), it keeps protons and neutrons bound together, rather than letting the repulsion between positive protons break the nuclei apart.

When you get to nuclei the size of astatine and francium, the strong force has trouble holding all the protons and neutrons together. Francium has eighty-seven protons, none of which want to touch. Its 130-odd neutrons help to keep the positive charges apart, but they also add so much size that the strong force cannot reach all the way across a nucleus. This makes francium and astatine very unstable.

From all this, you may think that adding even more protons (in elements with atomic numbers greater than eight-seven) would make things even more unstable, and it does—sort of. But there's a catch. In the late 1940s, Maria Goeppert-Mayer developed a theory about long-lived "magic" elements—atoms with two, eight, twenty, twenty-eight, etc., protons or neutrons that were extrastable. Other numbers of protons or neutrons, such as ninety-two, also formed fairly stable nuclei, and that's why uranium is more stable than either astatine or francium, despite its being heavier. As you move down the periodic table element by element, then, things *generally* get less and less stable, but with some exceptions, as one force gains the upper hand, then the other.

In theory, magic numbers extend until infinity, and it turned out that there was a semistable nucleus after uranium, at element 114, flerovium. Just as strangely, elements such as copernicium and livermorium seemed (on paper, at least) to also be somewhat stable since they had *close* to 114 protons. Even being close to a magic number seems to help. Scientists began calling this cluster of elements the "island of stability."

Element 87, francium, is stranded between a magic nucleus at 82 and a somewhat stable nucleus at 92. Francium is not only the least stable natural element, it's less stable than every element up to 104.

Still, there's more francium than astatine. Why? Because many radioactive elements around uranium happen to decay *into* francium as they disintegrate. But francium, instead of doing the normal alpha decay and thereby converting itself (through the loss of two protons) into astatine, decides more than 99.9 percent of the time to undergo beta decay instead and become radium.

Radium then undergoes a bunch of alpha decays that leap over astatine. In other words, the path of many decaying atoms leads to a short layover on francium—hence the twenty to thirty ounces of it. At the same time, francium shuttles atoms away from astatine, causing astatine to remain very rare.

So what about that island of stability? It's doubtful that chemists will ever make elements with very high magic numbers. But element 114 was confirmed and christened flerovium in 2012, so perhaps they can make a stable element 126 and go from there. Maybe even elements in the 140s, 160s, and 180s are possible, and if so, then the island of stability would become a chain of islands.

The thrilling part is that those new elements, instead of being just heavier versions of what we already know, could have weird and wonderful new properties.

REIMAGINING THE TABLE

And if they are ever made, the standard castles-with-turrets look of our table, printed in the back of every chemistry book, is just one possible arrangement of elements—maybe there will be a new look to the table in the future. Many of our grandparents grew up with quite a different table, one just eight columns wide all the way down. It looked more like a calendar, with all the rows of the transition metals crammed into half boxes, like those unfortunate 30s and 31s in awkwardly arranged months. A few people even shoved the lanthanides into the main body of the table, creating a crowded mess.

No one thought to give the transition metals a little more space until Glenn Seaborg and his colleagues made over the entire periodic table between the late 1930s and early 1960s. It wasn't just that they added elements. They also realized that elements like actinium (element 89) didn't fit into the scheme that they'd grown up with.

Actinium was the key element in giving the modern periodic table its shape, since Seaborg and his colleagues decided to place all the heavy elements known at the time—now called the actinides—at the bottom of the table. As long as they were moving those elements, they decided to give the transition metals more elbow room, too, and instead of cramming them into triangles, they added ten columns to the table. This blueprint made so much sense that many people copied Seaborg. It took a while, but in the 1970s the periodic calendar finally shifted to become the periodic castle that we have today.

But who says that's the ideal shape? The columns have dominated since Mendeleev's day, but Mendeleev himself designed thirty different periodic tables, and by the 1970s, scientists had designed more than seven hundred variations. Some chemists fuss with hydrogen and helium, dropping them into different columns. One clever modern periodic table looks like a honeycomb, with each hexagonal box spiraling outward in wider and wider arms from the hydrogen core. Other versions have a hydrogen "sun" at the center of the table, and all the other elements orbit it like planets with moons. Some have mapped the periodic table onto helixes, like our DNA, or sketched out periodic tables where rows and columns double back on themselves and wrap around the paper. We don't even have to limit periodic tables to two dimensions anymore.

In the end, though, there's little doubt that Seaborg's table of rows and turrets, with the lanthanides and actinides like moats along the bottom, will dominate chemistry classes for generations to come. It's a good combination of easy to make and easy to learn. But it's a shame more textbook publishers don't balance Seaborg's table with a few of the weirder periodic table arrangements: 3-D shapes that pop up and buckle on the page and bend far-distant elements nearer to each other, sparking some link in the imagination when you finally see them side by side.

I wish very much that I could donate $1,000 to some nonprofit group to support messing with wild new periodic tables based on whatever organizing ideas people can imagine. The current periodic table has served us well so far, but reimagining it and re-creating it are important for humans.

Truly Universal

If aliens ever land and park here, there's no guarantee we'll be able to communicate with them or explain our primary concerns to them—would they even understand concepts like love, religion, respect, family, peace? Probably the only thing they'll be able to grasp are numbers like pi and...the properties of the periodic table. I want them to be impressed with our ingenuity in organizing those properties. And maybe, just maybe, for them to see some shape they recognize among our collection.

Then again, our good old boxy array of rows and turrets, with its marvelous, clean shape, has served us pretty well so far. It has unlocked the science of everything from stars to giant shark teeth, from medicine to natural nuclear reactors. And there are still new discoveries being made—in both the human and the scientific realms. The periodic table is the basis of so many discoveries in chemistry and physics and biology, and it's one of the few things we know of that's literally universal—something that even alien life-forms would understand. But the periodic table of the elements is a very human thing as well, a treasure trove of all our passions and obsessions. And I'm constantly amazed at all we've managed to pack in there.

ACKNOWLEDGMENTS

Writing *The Disappearing Spoon* was a life-changing experience for me, and I'm thrilled to bring all the magic of the periodic table to young readers. I can't think of anything more worthwhile than unlocking the wonders of the table for the next generation. But this book wouldn't be here without the hard work and dedication of many people. First of all, I'd like to thank the editor of this edition, Farrin Jacobs, who saw the potential the book had for young readers and who has guided it since the beginning. Without her invaluable suggestions, the book wouldn't have happened. I'd also like to thank the adapters, Adrian Dingle and Kelsey Kennedy, who shaped and crafted the text and made the periodic table come alive all over again. It goes without saying that I'm indebted once more to all the incredible designers at Little, Brown who made the book pop, and all the copy editors there who saved me from blunders. Finally, I'd like to thank my own young readers—my niece and nephew, Penny and Harry.

PERIODIC TABLE

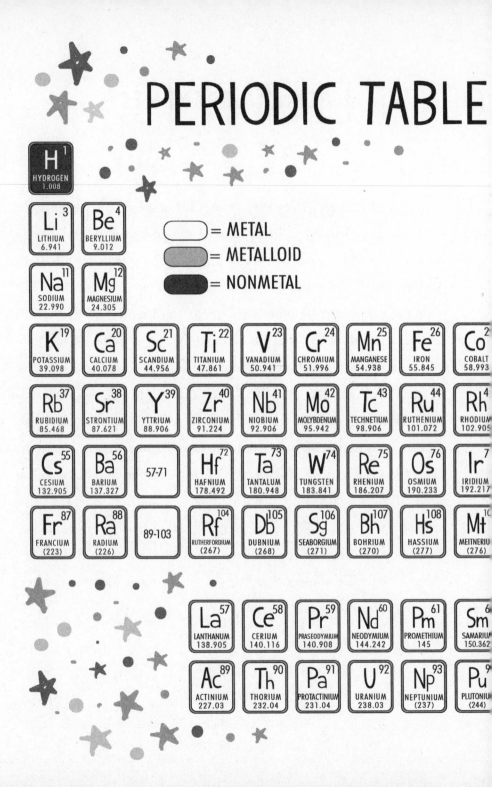

H¹ HYDROGEN 1.008	

= METAL
= METALLOID
= NONMETAL

Li³ LITHIUM 6.941	Be⁴ BERYLLIUM 9.012
Na¹¹ SODIUM 22.990	Mg¹² MAGNESIUM 24.305

K¹⁹ POTASSIUM 39.098	Ca²⁰ CALCIUM 40.078	Sc²¹ SCANDIUM 44.956	Ti²² TITANIUM 47.861	V²³ VANADIUM 50.941	Cr²⁴ CHROMIUM 51.996	Mn²⁵ MANGANESE 54.938	Fe²⁶ IRON 55.845	Co² COBALT 58.993
Rb³⁷ RUBIDIUM 85.468	Sr³⁸ STRONTIUM 87.621	Y³⁹ YTTRIUM 88.906	Zr⁴⁰ ZIRCONIUM 91.224	Nb⁴¹ NIOBIUM 92.906	Mo⁴² MOLYBDENUM 95.942	Tc⁴³ TECHNETIUM 98.906	Ru⁴⁴ RUTHENIUM 101.072	Rh⁴ RHODIUM 102.905
Cs⁵⁵ CESIUM 132.905	Ba⁵⁶ BARIUM 137.327	57-71	Hf⁷² HAFNIUM 178.492	Ta⁷³ TANTALUM 180.948	W⁷⁴ TUNGSTEN 183.841	Re⁷⁵ RHENIUM 186.207	Os⁷⁶ OSMIUM 190.233	Ir⁷ IRIDIUM 192.217
Fr⁸⁷ FRANCIUM (223)	Ra⁸⁸ RADIUM (226)	89-103	Rf¹⁰⁴ RUTHERFORDIUM (267)	Db¹⁰⁵ DUBNIUM (268)	Sg¹⁰⁶ SEABORGIUM (271)	Bh¹⁰⁷ BOHRIUM (270)	Hs¹⁰⁸ HASSIUM (277)	Mt¹⁰ MEITNERIUM (276)

La⁵⁷ LANTHANUM 138.905	Ce⁵⁸ CERIUM 140.116	Pr⁵⁹ PRASEODYMIUM 140.908	Nd⁶⁰ NEODYMIUM 144.242	Pm⁶¹ PROMETHIUM 145	Sm⁶ SAMARIUM 150.362
Ac⁸⁹ ACTINIUM 227.03	Th⁹⁰ THORIUM 232.04	Pa⁹¹ PROTACTINIUM 231.04	U⁹² URANIUM 238.03	Np⁹³ NEPTUNIUM (237)	Pu PLUTONIUM (244)

OF THE ELEMENTS

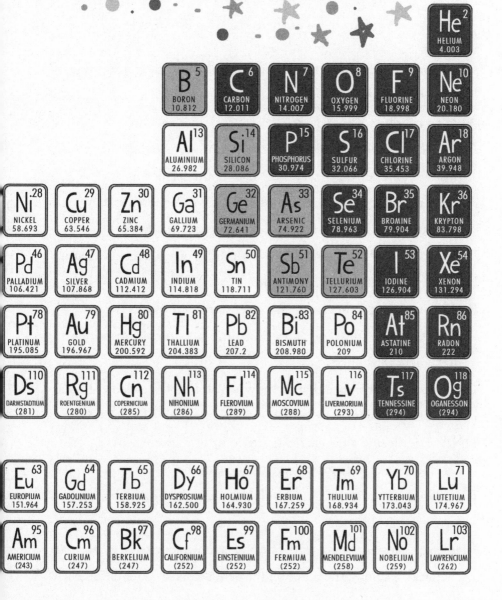

					He 2 HELIUM 4.003
B 5 BORON 10.812	C 6 CARBON 12.011	N 7 NITROGEN 14.007	O 8 OXYGEN 15.999	F 9 FLUORINE 18.998	Ne 10 NEON 20.180
Al 13 ALUMINIUM 26.982	Si 14 SILICON 28.086	P 15 PHOSPHORUS 30.974	S 16 SULFUR 32.066	Cl 17 CHLORINE 35.453	Ar 18 ARGON 39.948

Ni 28 NICKEL 58.693	Cu 29 COPPER 63.546	Zn 30 ZINC 65.384	Ga 31 GALLIUM 69.723	Ge 32 GERMANIUM 72.641	As 33 ARSENIC 74.922	Se 34 SELENIUM 78.963	Br 35 BROMINE 79.904	Kr 36 KRYPTON 83.798
Pd 46 PALLADIUM 106.421	Ag 47 SILVER 107.868	Cd 48 CADMIUM 112.412	In 49 INDIUM 114.818	Sn 50 TIN 118.711	Sb 51 ANTIMONY 121.760	Te 52 TELLURIUM 127.603	I 53 IODINE 126.904	Xe 54 XENON 131.294
Pt 78 PLATINUM 195.085	Au 79 GOLD 196.967	Hg 80 MERCURY 200.592	Tl 81 THALLIUM 204.383	Pb 82 LEAD 207.2	Bi 83 BISMUTH 208.980	Po 84 POLONIUM 209	At 85 ASTATINE 210	Rn 86 RADON 222
Ds 110 DARMSTADTIUM (281)	Rg 111 ROENTGENIUM (280)	Cn 112 COPERNICIUM (285)	Nh 113 NIHONIUM (286)	Fl 114 FLEROVIUM (289)	Mc 115 MOSCOVIUM (288)	Lv 116 LIVERMORIUM (293)	Ts 117 TENNESSINE (294)	Og 118 OGANESSON (294)

Eu 63 EUROPIUM 151.964	Gd 64 GADOLINIUM 157.253	Tb 65 TERBIUM 158.925	Dy 66 DYSPROSIUM 162.500	Ho 67 HOLMIUM 164.930	Er 68 ERBIUM 167.259	Tm 69 THULIUM 168.934	Yb 70 YTTERBIUM 173.043	Lu 71 LUTETIUM 174.967
Am 95 AMERICIUM (243)	Cm 96 CURIUM (247)	Bk 97 BERKELIUM (247)	Cf 98 CALIFORNIUM (252)	Es 99 EINSTEINIUM (252)	Fm 100 FERMIUM (252)	Md 101 MENDELEVIUM (258)	No 102 NOBELIUM (259)	Lr 103 LAWRENCIUM (262)

GLOSSARY

Alkali metal: extremely reactive elements found in column one of the periodic table

Alloy: a mixture of metals

Atom: the smallest particle of an element, consisting of protons, neutrons, and electrons; atoms make up molecules

Atomic number: the number of protons in an element, which determines its identity and place on the periodic table

Atomic weight: the average weight of all atoms of an element in nature

Biology: the study of living creatures

Bond: a connection between two atoms, formed by electrons

Chemistry: the study of atoms forming and breaking bonds to make new substances

Compound: a substance that forms when atoms of one element bond with atoms of another element; examples include H_2O or CO_2

DNA: a molecule that carries genetic information in living creatures (DNA stands for deoxyribonucleic acid)

Electron: a negative particle inside atoms; atoms share electrons to form chemical bonds

Element: a substance that cannot be broken down or altered by normal, chemical reactions; the boxes on the periodic table contain elements

Halogen: an energetic and reactive element in column seventeen of the periodic table

Ion: a charged atom, either positive or negative

Isotope: atoms of the same element with the same atomic number but different weights; in other words, atoms with the same number of protons but different number of neutrons

Molecule: particle formed when two or more atoms bond together; also, the smallest particle of a substance that has all the properties of the substance

Neutron: a particle inside the atomic nucleus without a charge

Noble gas: an element that tends to not react with other elements because it already has all the electrons it needs; found in column eighteen of the periodic table

Nucleus: the tiny core of an atom, which remains unchanged in a chemical reaction

Particle: a catch-all term for basic units of matter such as atoms, protons, or electrons

Physics: the study of the properties of matter and energy

Proton: a positive particle in the atomic nucleus

Quantum mechanics: the study of how subatomic particles behave, often in bizarre ways

Radioactive atom: unstable atom whose nucleus decays or splits, allowing the atom to change identity and become another element

Transmutation: the changing of one element into another

BIBLIOGRAPHY

These were far from the only books I consulted during my research. These were simply the best books for a general audience, if you want to know more about the periodic table or various elements on it.

Coffey, Patrick. *Cathedrals of Science: The Personalities and Rivalries That Made Modern Chemistry.* New York: Oxford University Press, 2008.

Emsley, John. *Nature's Building Blocks: An A–Z Guide to the Elements.* New York: Oxford University Press, 2003.

Jones, Sheilla. *The Quantum Ten: A Story of Passion, Tragedy, Ambition, and Science.* New York: Oxford University Press, 2008.

Reid, T. R. *The Chip: How Two Americans Invented the Microchip and Launched a Revolution.* New York: Random House, 2001.

Rhodes, Richard. *The Making of the Atomic Bomb.* New York: Simon & Schuster, 1995.

Sacks, Oliver. *Awakenings.* New York: Vintage, 1999.

Scerri, Eric. *The Periodic Table: Its Story and Its Significance.* New York: Oxford University Press, 2006.

Seaborg, Glenn, and Eric Seaborg. *Adventures in the Atomic Age: From Watts to Washington*. New York: Farrar, Straus and Giroux, 2001.

Zoellner, Tom. *Uranium: War, Energy, and the Rock That Shaped the Earth*. New York: Viking, 2009.

INDEX